AR and VR Using the WebXR API

Learn to Create Immersive Content with WebGL, Three.js, and A-Frame

Rakesh Baruah

Apress®

AR and VR Using the WebXR API

Rakesh Baruah
Brookfield, WI, USA

ISBN-13 (pbk): 978-1-4842-6317-4   ISBN-13 (electronic): 978-1-4842-6318-1
https://doi.org/10.1007/978-1-4842-6318-1

Managing Director, Apress Media LLC: Welmoed Spahr
Acquisitions Editor: Spandana Chatterjee
Development Editor: James Markham
Coordinating Editor: Divya Modi

Cover designed by eStudioCalamar

Cover image designed by Pixabay

Distributed to the book trade worldwide by Springer Science+Business Media New York, 1 New York Plaza, Suite 4600, New York, NY 10004-1562, USA. Phone 1-800-SPRINGER, fax (201) 348-4505, e-mail orders-ny@springer-sbm.com, or visit www.springeronline.com. Apress Media, LLC is a California LLC and the sole member (owner) is Springer Science + Business Media Finance Inc (SSBM Finance Inc). SSBM Finance Inc is a **Delaware** corporation.

For information on translations, please e-mail booktranslations@springernature.com; for reprint, paperback, or audio rights, please e-mail bookpermissions@springernature.com.

Apress titles may be purchased in bulk for academic, corporate, or promotional use. eBook versions and licenses are also available for most titles. For more information, reference our Print and eBook Bulk Sales web page at http://www.apress.com/bulk-sales.

Any source code or other supplementary material referenced by the author in this book is available to readers on GitHub via the book's product page, located at www.apress.com/ 978-1-4842-6317-4. For more detailed information, please visit www.apress.com/source-code.

Printed on acid-free paper

To Mom & Dad for boundless patience, love, and support

Table of Contents

About the Author

Rakesh Baruah is a writer and creator with 15 years of experience in new media, film, and television in New York City. After completing an MFA in screenwriting and directing for film from Columbia University, Rakesh joined the writers' room of a hit, primetime, network drama as an assistant. The experience opened his eyes to the limits of television and the opportunities promised by 3D, immersive content. In 2016 he began a self-guided journey toward mixed reality design that has taken him through startups, boot camps, the Microsoft offices, and many, many hours in front of a computer. He is the author of one previous book on virtual reality and the Unity Game Engine and has received an Nvidia-certified nanodegree in Computer Vision. He currently teaches high school computer science in Milwaukee, WI. He shares what he's learned with you in a style and format designed specifically for the person who, in high school, preferred English class to Trigonometry.

About the Technical Reviewer

 **Yogendra Sharma** is a developer with experience in architecture, design, and development of scalable and distributed applications, with a core interest in Microservices and DevOps. He is currently working as an IoT and Cloud Architect at Intelizign Engineering Services Pvt Pune. He also has hands-on experience in technologies such as AR/VR, CAD CAM, Simulation, AWS, IoT, Python, J2SE, J2EE, NodeJS, VueJs, Angular, MongoDB, and Docker. He constantly explores technical novelties, and he is open-minded and eager to learn about new technologies and frameworks. He has reviewed several books and video courses published by Packt and Apress.

Acknowledgments

Deep thanks to the members of the Immersive Web Working Group for their support of the WebXR API. To Brandon Jones, Nell, Manish, and others whom I only know through Twitter, thank you for the attention you put into the documentation for the WebXR API and all of its features. Mr. Doob, thanks go to you and your compatriots for creating and maintaining Three.js. To the team at Google Chrome Labs, thank you for evangelizing the promise of augmented reality on the Web. To Mozilla and all who have called it an employer, thank you for everything you have done to help make the Web a more inclusive, democratic space. Thank you to the team members at Mozilla Mixed Reality, Mozilla Hubs, MDN, and A-Frame for creating, supporting, and maintaining the tools to make mobile mixed reality an opportunity for everyone in the world. An incredibly special thank you to my team at Apress for their tireless devotion to my project. Spandana Chatterjee, thank you for your support and concern for all things book related and not. James Markham, thank you for the guidance you have provided for each chapter. To Yogendra Sharma, my technical editor, thank you for keen eyes and a sharp mind that kept me honest. And finally, thank you to my primary editor, Divya Modi, for whom this is my second book. Divya, thank you for the prompt responses, clarifications, follow-ups, and forwards that made collaborating remotely a smooth, fruitful experience.

Introduction

This book is a resource to help you become familiar with the tools to create mobile mixed reality for the Web. On July 24, 2020 the World Wide Web Consortium, the international standards organization for the World Wide Web, published its most recent version, as of this writing, of the WebXR API specification. The specification describes how Web browsers can implement support for virtual and augmented reality devices, including headsets and sensors, on the Web. The first iteration of the specification appeared in 2017 as the WebVR API. However, in 2018 the expansion of use cases for VR and AR on the Web prompted the Immersive Web Working Group—made up of contributors from Google, Microsoft, Mozilla, and elsewhere—to overhaul WebVR in favor of an API designed to embrace what the future of mixed reality may offer. By June of 2020, at least four of the leading Web browsers, including Google Chrome, Microsoft Edge, Mozilla Firefox, and Oculus Browser, provided support for the WebXR API.

As WebXR is a new, evolving specification, resources for its development are sparse. In this book I have created a pathway to help you prepare for the future of mobile, mixed reality development. By the book's end you will be familiar with the most common tools used for WebXR development today. These tools include Visual Studio Code, WebGL, Three.js, and A-Frame. Familiarity with HTML, CSS, and JavaScript is not required to benefit from the lessons in this book.

What follows is a road map for the rest of the course. Chapter 1 introduces the concepts behind the WebXR API as well as the tools you may need to begin developing mobile, immersive applications. Chapter 2 places us at the point of origin for 3D graphics on the Web, WebGL. By creating simple projects with WebGL, HTML, and JavaScript, you will quickly learn the fundamentals of how the WebXR API works inside a browser. In Chapter 3 we remain with WebGL, as its bare-bones syntax makes clear the ins and outs of the graphics rendering pipeline that connects server, client, and GPU. Chapter 4 builds on the preceding two chapters, culminating with an explanation of linear algebra through WebGL. The simple, yet important, principles of linear algebra covered in Chapter 4 provide the suggested groundwork for a deep dive into immersive Web development with the 3D JavaScript library, Three.js, in Chapter 5. With a thorough understanding of the WebGL pipeline and the convenience created by the Three.js library, you will create a virtual reality project on your local machine and load it into a VR-capable device through the Internet via the WebXR API in Chapter 6. Chapter 7 moves the focus from virtual reality to augmented reality programming with Three. js. Using the features of the WebXR API's Augmented Reality module, Chapter 7 provides steps toward creating mobile AR experiences that include animation and user interaction. Chapter 8 returns to the topic of virtual reality to introduce the use of A-Frame, a framework for creating mobile XR experiences using Three.js. Both Chapters 9 and 10 remain with A-Frame, as Chapter 9 explains how to implement real-world physics and user interaction in a VR scene through the WebXR API's implementation of the Gamepad API, also built into many browsers. Finally, Chapter 10 provides instruction on how to import 3D models into A-Frame, animate them, and view them in augmented reality through GitHub Pages.

The WebXR API is poised to become a useful tool for XR and Web developers alike. As the lines between mobile and native, augmented and virtual blur, applications that make use of both 2D and immersive technologies will become more common. I have created the lessons inside this book with the intent to help you join the growing community of developers designing experiences for the immersive Web. No prior experience with Web development or 3D programming is assumed. As the WebXR API is such a new technology, more seasoned developers may also benefit from the instruction contained within. As the future of

Web development moves into a third dimension and the principles of game development move on to the Web, more opportunities will open up for creative minds to forge the language of the new Internet. I hope you, empowered with the lessons in this course, will be among those leading the charge.

CHAPTER 1

Getting Started

WebXR is not a programming language; it's not even a library of code we can access to create our apps. WebXR is a specification developed by the World Wide Web Consortium, W3C, a nonprofit group of industry experts who collaborate to create standard protocols across the Web. The W3C has left the implementation of the WebXR guidelines to the developers of browsers. WebXR, therefore, is nothing more than a set of rules agreed upon by industry.

Not to be confused with the WebXR specification, the WebXR API is an *implementation* of the WebXR feature set. The WebXR API serves as an interface between XR Web content and the devices on which they run. For example, the WebXR API collects data regarding the orientation of a headset and a user's pose. The WebXR API provides developers access to user data through its library of commands.

Yet, the WebXR Device API does have important limitations: it can't manage 3D data or draw anything to a screen. The WebXR API is not a rendering engine. It cannot load models, wrap them in textures, and paint them to pixels—a process known as rasterization. To rasterize 3D content in a browser, the WebXR API extends another API called WebGL.

Following an introduction to the components integral to the use of the WebXR API, we will discuss the tools we need to create XR applications of our own. The tools required for creating WebXR applications are a code editor, a local development server, a Web browser, and an XR device. Developers without access to an XR device may use the WebXR Emulator provided by browser creators like Mozilla. All of these are discussed in a later section of this chapter.

© Rakesh Baruah 2021
R. Baruah, *AR and VR Using the WebXR API*,
https://doi.org/10.1007/978-1-4842-6318-1_1

A thorough understanding of how the WebXR API builds upon the fundamental features of the Web browser will make understanding the tools we will use later in the course, such as the Three.js JavaScript library and the A-Frame framework, an easier process. By preparing ourselves with an understanding of the WebXR API from the ground up and a knowledge of how the tools we will use will impact the development of our WebXR apps, we will guarantee that we are best prepared to meet whatever advancements the WebXR API may release in the future.

In this chapter you will:

- Learn the origin and purpose of WebGL

- Briefly cover the role of JavaScript in the history of the Web browser

- Learn the purpose of the browser's rendering engine

- Learn the role played by buffers in XR applications

- Learn the value that graphics processing units (GPUs) offer to creating and running XR apps

- Survey the tools needed to create WebXR applications

- Cover the system requirements for the use of these tools

- Come to understand the suite of technologies used throughout this course

WebGL

WebGL is a Web graphics library available through a JavaScript API in all contemporary Web browsers. Like the WebXR API, the WebGL API also conforms to a specification. The specification for WebGL, however, is not maintained by the W3C, but by a different consortium known as the Kronos Group. Comprising over 150 leading technology companies, the

Kronos group promotes advanced Web standards for graphics, mixed reality, and machine learning applications. One among their many visual computing APIs is the OpenGL graphics standard.

The OpenGL graphics standard specifies a protocol for communication between an application and the drivers of a GPU, such as those made by Nvidia and AMD. While OpenGL is compatible across machines, platform-specific APIs like Microsoft's DirectX and Apple's Metal also exist. However, OpenGL's cross-platform applicability has made its younger cousin, OpenGL ES, a popular graphics API to implement on mobile devices. The ES in OpenGL ES stands for "embedded systems," which means the API targets small, low-power devices. As these devices cannot avail themselves of the big GPUs you can find in a desktop gaming computer, for example, they require a graphics API dedicated to their specific needs.

OpenGL ES' ability to operate on mobile devices allows WebGL to create 2D and 3D graphics in Web browsers running on stand-alone headsets and smartphones. It is the Kronos Group's specification for OpenGL ES that informs the implementation of the WebGL API. While the communication between applications and GPUs still requires the use of GLSL, the language of OpenGL's rendering and drawing commands, the WebGL API enables Web developers to blend GLSL with a language they are much more comfortable with, JavaScript. After all, JavaScript is the language of the Web, and the Web is the domain of the browser.

The Browser

The Web browser as we know it today really came of age in 1995 with the release of Netscape Navigator. Though Netscape eventually succumbed to the industry leviathan of Microsoft's Internet Explorer, its legacy continues to inform the nature of the Web. But Netscape wasn't even the first publicly used Web browser. That distinction belongs to an earlier iteration of Navigator called Mosaic. In fact, Navigator and its predecessor had been around since 1993. What, then, happened in 1995 to mark the year as a watershed moment in the browser wars?

JavaScript happened. While developing Navigator, Netscape sought
a scripting language to use inside its browser. Originally, developers at
Netscape wanted a programming language that embraced the object-
oriented paradigm (OOP) of Java. However, the OOP nature of Java proved
ill-fitting for the needs of the browser. Looking for outside help, Netscape
recruited software engineer Brendan Eich to implement a version of the
Scheme programming language for the browser. For better or worse, the
minimalist dialect of Scheme didn't appeal to the larger community of
developers who preferred Java's OOP approach to software design. Looking
for a compromise, Netscape brass asked Eich to strike a balance between
the structure of Java and the flexibility of Scheme. As the apocryphal story
goes, Eich developed what came to be known as JavaScript over the course
of just 10 days.

Eich's intent with JavaScript was to "touch the page." By any measure
Eich succeeded, as JavaScript is one of the most popular programming
languages used worldwide. Web developers have used JavaScript and
members of its family like AJAX and JQuery for decades to create Web
applications increasingly more responsive to user feedback. With the
arrival of Node.js, JavaScript leapt from the front end to the server-side back
end of Web development, an arena once exclusively dominated by more
established languages like C and C++. JavaScript's flexibility has made it a
go-to language for many developers interested in designing for the full stack.
But its efficacy may not be more apparent than in the Web browser, where its
extensibility allows for the creation of streaming XR content.

The browser is literally our window into the World Wide Web. One
need not do more than execute the function window.onLoad() in a
JavaScript file to understand what I mean. Really, though, the Web browser
is less a window than a wall. It doesn't allow us to peer into the Web.
Rather, it brings the Web into our homes, onto our tablets and our phones,
by painting the contents of the Web onto the screens of our devices. About
60 times a second a Web browser repaints itself to create the illusion of a
world that we surf with keyboard strokes and mouse clicks. The core of a

Web browser's functionality is its ability to render remote content to our screens. The source of this power is the product of one of its two main engines.

The Render Engine

Two engines make up the modern Web browser application. One is the JavaScript engine, such as Chrome's V8 engine, which manages the compilation of JavaScript code. The other is the engine of primary importance to us, at this point in our journey. That engine is the one responsible for rendering content delivered from a server to our screens.

When information arrives at our Internet-connected devices, it passes through the many protocol layers of the network specification before appearing inside our browsing window. Data leaves a server wrapped in layers of instructions that communicate to each node on the network how to route data to its target. Layer by layer is stripped away by network nodes until the data packet reaches the machine of the client who requested it.

If the header of the data packet matches what the browser expects, then the browser gets to work refitting the data to appear on our screen as it began at its source. Employing its ability to parse the packet's content, the browser builds a page from the syntax of its HTML document. While the JavaScript engine attends to the demands of the website's JavaScript modules, the browser's rendering engine digs into the layout and compositing instructions described through HTML and CSS. When the rendering engine is through laying out the elements of a page and painting them in the order they appear on the screen, we, the user of the client browser, will have barely noticed that any time has passed at all.

But how exactly does a browser understand where on our screens it should draw certain shapes or tint certain pixels? Sure, a designer has included the instruction set for a page's appearance in HTML and CSS, but what if a user scrolls? Enters a character into a form? Or presses play on a video? A browser requires a place to store in memory the content it receives from a server to repaint to the page in case of update. The server too needs memory to hold data in queue as it waits to stream to the browser. What are these objects of memory called?

Buffers

If you've ever tapped your foot impatiently waiting for a Web page to load, then you're already familiar with the concept behind a buffer. Buffers are slots of memory included in hardware to hold information in bits. Buffers include addresses that inform pointers in software programs of the location of important data. Programs retrieve data from buffers before passing it through a thread on a processing unit to undergo operations. If the amount of data to move is greater than the volume, or capacity, of a thread, then a program's execution will lag. If the data are the bits of a YouTube video, then you're going to tap your foot as you wait for it to load.

Buffers are registers for memory allocation. They exist on processors, on hard drives, in RAM, and even virtually in the browser as cache. Much of creating XR for the Web relies on the efficient storing and retrieving of data from buffers; they are an important part of the WebGL specification. Transferring data to and from buffers can be costly and can destroy the believability of an immersive experience if causing lag. Fortunately, the rapid filling and emptying of buffers has been significantly improved by the increasing availability of desktop and mobile GPUs.

The Graphics Processing Unit

GPUs are computer chips that specialize in parallel processing. CPUs, central processing units, are the brain of computing devices. Their embedded logic gates and internal clocks are the essence of digital computing. Over time, CPUs have increased their productivity through the inclusion of more cores. Broadly speaking, cores on a CPU align with the number of processes a chip can run at the same time. More cores mean more threads, which mean a greater capacity of the computer to execute tasks concurrently. The number of cores serves as a benchmark for the speed of a processor. Whereas higher-end CPUs can have somewhere around eight cores, consumer-grade GPUs can have anywhere from the hundreds to the thousands.

Today GPUs power much of the intensive computing required by AI applications in industries as far and wide as self-driving cars to protein synthesis. Their popularity, however, grew because of the breakthroughs made by designers of video games. Like the Web browser, video game applications paint and repaint a screen up to hundreds of times a second. Each frame update requires calculations of character positions, environment, lighting, cameras, materials, textures, and more. The faster and more detailed a game, the higher the demand on a machine's rendering power. Applications implementing the specifications of OpenGL, such as Microsoft's DirectX, leveraged the parallel processing of GPUs and their many, many cores to create video games that could compute and render complex character geometry at rates and volumes never before seen.

As the prevalence of GPUs in consumer machines has grown, so too have the availability and demand for virtual reality content. The speed at which GPUs can calculate the shape, color, position, and orientation of objects to a screen has supported the beginning of a new era in 3D graphics. Contemporary techniques for rendering through GPU computation, such as raytracing, have blurred the line between the real and virtual in ways that are equally exciting and unsettling. But the evolution of GPU tech isn't limited to beefy consoles and gaming PCs. Advancements in engineering and chip design have shrunk the power of GPUs to the nanometer scale, bringing the wonder of 3D to mobile and handheld devices.

The Present Future

Chipsets in modern mobile VR headsets and smartphones are pushing the envelope of what has been possible to achieve through computing. As the parallel execution of GPUs and newer system architectures arrive on more and smaller devices, the demands placed on machines to render XR content in real time will become less daunting. The WebXR API, by extending the WebGL API (which is itself based on the specifications of OpenGL ES), allows us as XR content creators to leverage the power of GPUs to bring virtual and augmented experiences to hundreds of millions of people through the Internet.

In designing JavaScript, Brendan Eich may have aimed to give designers the ability to touch the page of a website. Twenty-five years later JavaScript endures, and through the WebXR API in the browser, provides us, designers, with the ability to touch reality itself. In the remainder of the chapter you will learn the tools required to build XR content with the WebXR API.

Tooling Up

The tools described in the following sections have proved helpful to me during my development of WebXR content. Some are required; others are not. Each has been vetted by reputable parties if not directly by me. As always should be the case when creating with a bleeding edge technology like WebXR, refer to the most recent, published documentation for up-to-date compatibility and requirements.

A Code Editor

Like a text editor, a code editor allows you to type the syntax of a program into a document. Features built into a code editor create an environment convenient to writing, deploying, testing, and correcting code. Throughout this book I use Microsoft's Visual Studio Code editor (VS Code). It is cross-platform, popular, powerful, and free.

We will use it to write the HTML, JavaScript, and CSS required to create XR applications for the Web. As VS Code also includes a marketplace for convenient developer extensions and integration with GitHub's version control platform, it enjoys widespread popularity among developers of all stripes.

Visual Studio Code download requirements from Microsoft's documentation are as follows.

Hardware

Visual Studio Code is a small download (<100 MB) and has a disk footprint of 200 MB. VS Code is lightweight and should easily run on today's hardware.

We recommend:

- 1.6 GHz or faster processor
- 1 GB of RAM

Platforms

VS Code has been tested on the following platforms:

- OS X Yosemite
- Windows 7 (with .NET Framework 4.5.2), 8.0, 8.1, and 10 (32-bit and 64-bit)
- Linux (Debian): Ubuntu Desktop 14.04, Debian 7
- Linux (Red Hat): Red Hat Enterprise Linux 7, CentOS 7, Fedora 23

Additional Windows Requirements

Microsoft .NET Framework 4.5.2 is required for VS Code. If you are using Windows 7, please make sure .NET Framework 4.5.2 is installed.

Additional Linux requirements

- GLIBCXX version 3.4.15 or later

- GLIBC version 2.15 or later

For a list of the most recent requirements, visit: `https://code.visualstudio.com/Docs/supporting/requirements#_platforms`.

Local Web Server for Development

To test and debug Web applications written into a code editor, developers require the creation of a local Web server. Mimicking the behavior of a remote server that stores and delivers Web pages and their resources to client browsers, a local Web server allows developers to launch and view Web applications from their local machines. For the exercises in this book, I use the Live Server extension created by Ritwick Dey, available for free in the VS Code Extension Store.

Live Server VS Extension by Ritwick Dey

See `https://marketplace.visualstudio.com/items?itemName=ritwickdey.LiveServer`.

Other popular options to create a local Web server are modules available through Node.js and Python. Both Node and Python require installation on your machine before providing access to their local server resources.

NodeJS http-server Package from NPM

See www.npmjs.com/package/http-server.

Python HTTP server module

See https://docs.python.org/3/library/http.server.html.

Another common resource for the creation of a local development server is a program called Servez. Though I have not used it, I have read testimonials from other developers who speak favorably of its use for users not yet comfortable with local server deployment.

Servez— A Simple Web Server for Local Web Development

See https://greggman.github.io/servez/.

The list of options I have provided for the creation of a local development server is not exhaustive. Please use whatever solution you prefer, found here or elsewhere. **Do not** open the HTML and JavaScript files you create throughout this book directly from your machine's hard drive without the intermediate provided by a local Web server. Your use of a local Web server is **required** to complete the exercises in this book.

Regardless of the local development server you select, its use in the workflow presented in this course will be heavy. The local development server will operate as the interface between the programs we write in a code editor and the XR applications we see rendered onscreen.

A Web Browser Compatible with the WebXR API

As the WebXR API is a new interface, it does not yet enjoy wide support in Web browsers. The following Web browsers offer support for the WebXR API, as of this writing:

- Desktop/Laptop
    - Microsoft Edge
    - Google Chrome*
    - Mozilla Firefox**
- Mobile
    - Chrome for Android
    - Oculus Browser
    - Firefox Reality for Oculus Quest
    - Samsung Internet

    * Chrome versions compatible with WebXR:

```
https://immersive-web.github.io/webxr-reference/webxr-device-
api/compatibility.html
```

**See the section "WebXR Emulator."

For a current list of Web browsers compatible with the WebXR API, visit the Mozilla Developer Network documentation:

```
https://developer.mozilla.org/en-US/docs/Web/API/WebXR_Device_
API#Browser_compatibility
```

Of course, it comes as no surprise that to complete the exercises in this course you will need a Web browser. However, despite its ubiquity, the Web browser remains a powerful tool in the XR developer kit. In this course we will not only avail ourselves of a Web browser's integration with the WebXR API, but we will also make heavy use of its built-in developer tools, which allow us to test and troubleshoot our programs from within the browser itself.

XR Device

Though developing WebXR content does not require the use of an XR device, having one available is helpful for testing. Refer to the documentation provided by a device's manufacturer to enable the following:

- Developer mode

- USB-enabled debugging

Also, download whatever local and/or mobile applications the use of your device may require, as noted in the documentation for the device.

This book begins with exercises concerned exclusively with the browser, code editor, and GPU. However, the fundamentals we discuss in early chapters will form the foundation of later exercises using augmented and virtual reality features of the WebXR API. A VR headset, like an Oculus Quest or HTC Vive, and an AR-enabled phone will be handy tools to better understand how a user will experience the XR applications we write.

WebXR Emulator

Developers without access to an XR device may use the WebXR Emulator to test their applications. Created by the mixed reality team at the Mozilla foundation, the WebXR Emulator is a Web browser extension that enables developers to run and test XR content in a desktop browser without using a real XR device. The WebXR Emulator is available for the following browsers:

- Firefox:

  `https://addons.mozilla.org/en-US/firefox/addon/webxr-api-emulator/`

- Chrome: Available in the Google Chrome Web Store

- Other emulator options: While the Edge browser
  created by Microsoft does not, as of this writing, offer
  the WebXR Emulator extension, Microsoft does list its
  own emulator solutions in the Chromium DevTools
  section of their Edge documentation:

  `https://docs.microsoft.com/en-us/microsoft-edge/devtools-guide-chromium/device-mode/testing-other-browsers`

While we will not be discussing the use of the WebXR Emulator to test the XR applications we create in this book, the use of an emulator will be invaluable to anyone without access to an XR device.

Summary

The WebXR API is a specification created by the Immersive Web Working Group and maintained by the World Wide Web Consortium, WC3. Built upon the WebGL API, a specification that extends the OpenGL ES specification maintained by the Kronos Group, the WebXR API serves as the interface between WebXR applications and the XR devices used by users to access XR on the Web.

As a Web interface, the WebXR API makes full use of the features built into many, if not all, contemporary Web browsers. As developers, we access these features through the dominant scripting language of the Web: JavaScript. As an extension of the WebGL API, the WebXR API allows developers to merge the writing of applications in both JavaScript and

GLSL, the graphics library shading language supported by OpenGL ES. The WebXR API, therefore, is more than just an interface between developers and users of XR applications. Through the bridge it creates between WebGL and the drivers for GPUs built into computers and mobile devices alike, the WebXR API is also a conduit for client-server communication processed through the hundreds, and potentially thousands, of cores of a user's GPU(s).

Despite the WebXR API's breadth, reaching from software to hardware, from peripheral controllers to GPUs, the tools we need as developers of WebXR content are modest. A simple code editor, like Microsoft's Visual Studio Code, will provide us all the functionality we need to write HTML, CSS, JavaScript, and GLSL in a document; a development server, which we can download and access directly through Visual Studio Code, will provide the connection we need to run the applications we create on out computers; a Web browser, and its built-in developer tools, will not only allow us to load our applications, but also experience them through peripheral XR devices attached to our machines; further, a browser extension called the WebXR Emulator will allow developers without access to an XR device to troubleshoot and test their applications virtually; and finally, XR devices such as the Oculus Quest for virtual reality and an Android smartphone for augmented reality will enable to us to experience the mixed reality applications we create as if we are the users we intend to reach.

With the fundamental principles of the WebXR API's constituent parts and the tools we will need to make the most use of them under our belts, we are finally able to begin our time together as colearners of one of the most exciting consumer technologies available today, the WebXR API.

CHAPTER 2

Up and Running with WebGL

In the previous chapter we learned that WebGL is a low-level 2D and 3D graphics API implementing the Kronos Group specification for OpenGL ES in the Web browser. The "ES" in OpenGL ES abbreviates the term "embedded systems." By design, WebGL is optimized for devices such as phones and mobile headsets. The WebGL API enables developers to write JavaScript code with GLSL, the language used by OpenGL to run on graphics processors, to facilitate communication between a Web browser and a GPU.

As the WebGL API forms the foundation of the WebXR API, it is of value to understand what WebGL is and how it operates as an API in the Web browser. Familiarity with the WebGL API will allow for a deeper understanding of not only the WebXR API but also the tools available to create WebXR applications, like Three.js and A-Frame. As the progression of this book will move further into higher level abstractions of 3D graphics on the Web, it may become easy for you to get confused by all the low-level functionality hidden beneath convenience. With an understanding of how WebGL integrates between a Web browser and the GPU drivers of a user's machine, the performance of technologies introduced later will appear less as magic and more as simplifications of dense, repetitive logic.

© Rakesh Baruah 2021
R. Baruah, *AR and VR Using the WebXR API*,
https://doi.org/10.1007/978-1-4842-6318-1_2

In this chapter you will create a WebGL-enabled Web page with a code editor. In the process you will learn:

- The nature of an HTML document and its elements

- How to create a WebGL context

- The role of shaders in WebGL

- The roles of buffers and attributes in WebGL

- How shaders use the GPU to draw an image to a screen

The Form and Function of HTML

An HTML document is a collection of semantic tags that define the architecture of a Web page. Notable tags that define common sections of pages are called elements. Tags can be nested within each other to create complex, hierarchical relationships between elements in a Web page. The rendering engine of a browser parses the semantic tags in an HTML document to create a tree data structure that represents the formation of the page (Figure 2-1).

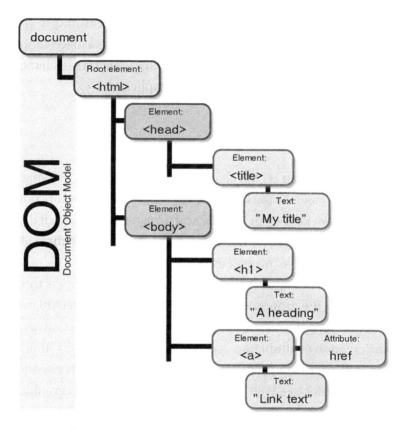

Figure 2-1. *The Document Object Model is a data structure that stores the elements of an HTML document in the form of a tree (Birger Eriksson 2012 CC BY-SA 3.0 https://en.wikipedia.org/ wiki/Document_Object_Model#/media/File:DOM-model.svg)*

The data structure of the tree provides JavaScript programs with the ability to touch and affect elements through traversal of the tree. In addition to semantic tags, HTML elements offer further classification with attributes, such as IDs and classes. The organization of an HTML page into a data structure accessible to a JavaScript program allows for the implementation of an interface called the Document Object Model (DOM) API (Figure 2-1). By serving as a connector between an HTML document and a JavaScript file, the DOM gives developers the opportunity to store a reference to an HTML element, manipulate the data presented within it, and update the element's appearance on the page. One HTML element is of primary importance to a WebGL-enabled application.

The Canvas

The Canvas element is an HTML element that allows for the drawing of graphics to a Web page. As the Canvas element is a container for content, it requires the use of JavaScript to draw and update the graphics it displays. Developers can draw to the Canvas element by creating code that calls methods made accessible through the Canvas API.

The Canvas API is a JavaScript library available to developers through the browser. Using the properties and functions in the Canvas API, we can draw colors and shapes on a Web page. Common uses of the Canvas API include the creation of animation, game graphics, data visualization, video processing, and photo manipulation. While the Canvas API is mostly used to render 2D graphics to a Web page, it allows us to create 3D graphics, too. We access the tools required to publish 3D content to the HTML canvas element through the browser's WebGL API.

In the following exercise you will use the Canvas and WebGL APIs to create a WebGL context that displays vertices and color drawn by the GPU into the browser window.

Exercise 1: Your First WebGL Application

The source code for this book is available on GitHub via the book's product page, located at www.apress.com/978-1-4842-6317-4.

A Reference to a Canvas

To begin creating a Web page featuring WebGL, we must first instruct the browser to provide us an area of the Web page on which we can draw our WebGL content.

First, create a new file in VS Code and save it as *index.html.* In the body of the document, type an exclamation point and press enter. The ! + ENTER shortcut should automatically generate an HTML template for a Web page.

```
<!DOCTYPE html>
<html lang="en">
<head>
    <meta charset="UTF-8">
    <meta name="viewport" content="width=device-width,
    initial-scale=1.0">
    <title>WebGL: Lesson 1</title>
</head>
<body>

</body>
</html>
```

The script tags in an HTML document inform the browser's layout engine of the structure of our page. The visual content rendered to the screen occurs between the <body> element tags of the HTML document. If you downloaded the Live Server extension from VS Code, then pressing ALT + L ALT + O will start a Web server on your local machine. Navigating to the address of the port in your browser, for example *localhost:5500*, will open the Web page on your screen.

To begin with, our Web page has nothing in it. We add content to the page by adding elements to the body of the HTML document.

```
<body>
    <canvas id="canvas"></canvas>
</body>
```

Even though we added a `<canvas>` element between the `<body>` tags of our HTML document, still nothing appears on the screen. Because in this exercise we aim to better understand the effects of the WebGL API in the browser, let's add color to the page using WebGL.

```
</body>
<script type="text/javascript">

</script>
</html>
```

Beneath the closing `<body>` tag in the *index.html* document in VS Code, add a `<script>` tag with a `type` attribute set to "`text/javascript`." As the element tags in an HTML document instruct the browser's layout engine on how to draw the elements to the user's screen, a `<script>` tag notifies the browser that what lies between is distinct from HTML. In this case, we've told the browser the text that will appear between the `<script>` tags will be of the type "`JavaScript`."

```
<script type="text/javascript">
    const canvas = document.querySelector("#c");
</script>
```

JavaScript provides us with the ability to manipulate the appearance of a Web page through the browser's DOM.

THE DOM

The DOM, or Document Object Model, is another JavaScript API provided to developers through the browser. Calling methods on the document object in JavaScript allow developers to dynamically change the appearance of a Web page by manipulating its HTML elements. The DOM is a data structure in the shape of a tree (Figure 2-1). Every element on the page hangs from the root of the DOM, the document object, as a leaf, otherwise known as a node. By arranging the content of a Web page in the structure of a tree, the browser's DOM API creates a useful interface for developers to conveniently touch different elements and their children nodes on a page.

By calling the querySelector() method on the document object with an argument referring to the *id* attribute on an HTML element, we can save a reference to the <canvas> element on the page in our JavaScript program.

VARIABLES

Like most programming languages, JavaScript stores data in memory that developers access through variables. Creating a variable with the *const* keyword notifies the browser that we will not need any more than the required amount of memory to store a <canvas> object, because we will not change its data type through the course of our program. Other keywords for variable creation include *var* and *let*. As each offers different features depending on their use in a program, we will address them when they appear in an exercise.

With a reference to the <canvas> element stored in our JavaScript program, we can access more functions available through the Canvas API.

```
const canvas = document.querySelector("#c");
const gl = canvas.getContext('webgl');
```

One function we can call on a Canvas object is the getContext() function. By passing in as an argument to the function the String 'webgl', we've instructed the browser to retrieve a WebGLRenderingContext and store it in the constant variable gl (Figure 2-2).

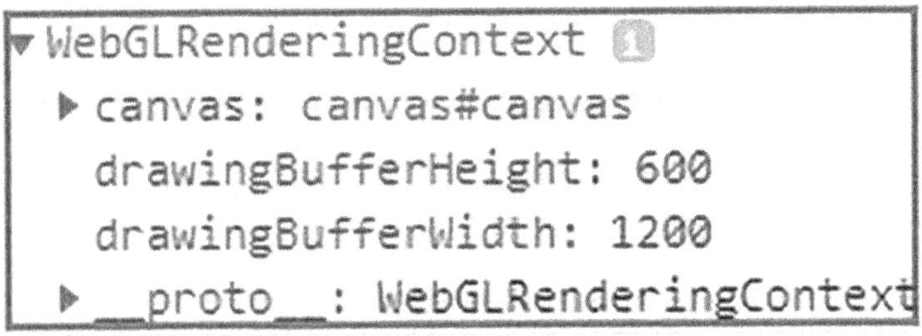

```
▼ WebGLRenderingContext 🔳
  ▶ canvas: canvas#canvas
    drawingBufferHeight: 600
    drawingBufferWidth: 1200
  ▶   proto   : WebGLRenderingContext
```

Figure 2-2. *Printing the value of the variable 'gl' to the browser's console shows that a call to an HTML canvas element's getContext() function with the parameter 'webgl' returns a WebGLRenderingContext, a feature built into the WebGL API*

The WebGL Context

The WebGLRenderingContext is the interface through which the browser accesses the functionality of the WebGL library. Once we have access to the WebGLRenderingContext in our application, we can render content to it.

```
const gl = canvas.getContext('webgl');
if (!gl) {
    console.log('WebGL unavailable');
} else {
    console.log('WebGL is good to go');
}
```

Of course, if a device or browser does not have the capability built into it to handle the requirements of WebGL, then the user will not be able to load the content of our page. To check whether a client, or user agent, can load WebGL content in their browser, we write an if/then conditional block in our JavaScript code. If the browser cannot return a WebGLRenderingContext, then the value of the gl variable will be null and the browser will write to its console the error message that we pass it. If the browser does return a WebGL context to the gl variable, then the browser's console will print a message of success.

Drawing on the WebGL Context

With a WebGLRenderingContext provided to our Web page, we now have the ability to use the WebGL API to draw to the canvas. Beneath the if/then conditional we created to handle error-checking, type the following:

```
    ...
    gl.clearColor(1, 0, 0, 1);
    gl.clear(gl.COLOR_BUFFER_BIT);
</script>
```

Calling the clearColor() method on the WebGLRenderingContext[1] object, gl, sets the default color of the canvas to the values of its arguments. We provide the clearColor() function with arguments in the form of a four-element vector. Collectively, the arguments comprise a vec4 data type. Each element refers to a normalized value of red, green, blue, and opacity. In this example, a value of 1 as the first argument defines a fully realized red value; the value of 1 as the final argument defines a fully realized opacity value, meaning the canvas will be completely opaque, as opposed to transparent.

---

[1]More information on the WebGLRenderingContext Object API can be found here: https://developer.mozilla.org/en-US/docs/Web/API/WebGLRendering Context

The `gl.clear()` method with a `gl.COLOR_BUFFER_BIT` argument instructs the rendering context to reset the color of the canvas to the value defined in the `clearColor()` function call. The `clearColor()` and `clear()` methods are predefined for us in the WebGL API.

Resizing the Canvas

If you're following along with the exercise, then you will see that the browser has filled our `<canvas>` element with the color red. Changing any of the values of the `gl.clearColor()` method to values between 0 and 1 will instruct the browser to paint the canvas differently. However, despite the `<canvas>` element occupying a branch of the document object, it only fills a small corner of the page. To change the default appearance of the `<canvas>` element, we must apply a style to it. One tool available to Web developers to style the appearance of HTML elements on a Web page is CSS.

An acronym for Cascading Style Sheets, CSS is the styling language of the Web. Whereas HTML is the markup language that defines the structure of a Web page, and JavaScript is the scripting language that manipulates the behavior of a Web page, CSS specifically targets a Web page's appearance.

```
<title>WebGL: Canvas Context</title>
<style>
    canvas {
        width: 640px;
        height: 480px;
        display: block;
    }
</style>
```

One way we can add CSS to a Web page is to include it between HTML <style> tags in the <head> section of an HTML document.

STYLING HTML ELEMENTS

CSS gains access to an element and its content on a Web page through the use of selectors. We can access basic HTML <elements> through simply typing their name, such as canvas. A specific element on a page can be accessed either through its id attribute with a hashtag or through its class attribute with a period preceding the class name.

Reloading the Web page after adding <canvas> styling properties and saving the HTML document in VS Code will draw the canvas to the screen with the pixel dimensions defined in the document <head>.

```
<style>
    canvas {
        width: 100vw;
        height: 100vh;
        display: block;
    }
</style>
```

Changing the width and height properties of the <canvas> element in CSS to values of 100vw and 100vh, respectively, will instruct the browser to draw the canvas as large as the browsing window will allow. Now the dimensions of the canvas will dynamically adjust to fill the width and height of the viewing window.

Shaders

At its core, WebGL is a library that provides resources to execute two tasks. One task collects the data of how a canvas context should appear to a user. The second task draws that data to the screen. We can understand these steps as State and Behavior, respectively. State is the position of points on a screen, their relationship to each other, and their color. Behavior is the series of operations performed by the GPU to render a WebGL application's state to the screen.

Shaders, in WebGL, refer to the functions we instruct the program to perform for every pixel in our canvas. WebGL includes two shaders: the vertex shader and the fragment shader. The vertex shader calculates the position of the points, or vertices, in a scene. The fragment shader calculates the values of the color each pixel should convey.

Source

As the vertex and fragment shader are only operations performed by the GPU, we must provide the data on which each shader will perform its operations. The data provided to a shader is called its source.

In your code editor, add the following text to the *index.html* document just beneath the <canvas> element in the <body> of the page:

```
...
<script id="vertex-data" type="not-javascript">

</script>

<script id="fragment-data" type="not-javascript">

</script>
</body>
```

As we learned earlier, the <script> tag element notifies the Web browser that the content that follows is not HTML. The type attribute conveys what kind of text occurs between the <script> brackets; it instructs the browser how to parse the content. The attribute "not-javascript" is not a standard of the specification; I've used it for clarity in this exercise.

```
<script id="vertex-source" type="not-javascript">
    attribute vec4 vertex_points;

    void main() {
        gl_Position = vertex_points;
    }
</script>
```

Adding the preceding to the body of the "vertex-source" script defines the vertex shader for the WebGL rendering context in the browser. The language of the vertex-source is GLSL, a C-style shading language for OpenGL. The content of the vertex-source in this example defines a vec4 datatype called "vertex_points" and passes it to the vertex shader's primary property, gl_Position, a variable built into WebGL that holds the coordinates for each vertex rendered to the screen.

```
<script id="fragment-source" type="not-javascript">
    precision mediump float;

    void main() {
        gl_FragColor = vec4(1.0, 0.0, 0.0, 1.0);
    }
</script>
```

Similarly, the data source for the fragment shader, written in GLSL, defines a `vec4` consisting of float, or decimal, values and saved to the WebGL fragment-shader property `gl_FragColor`. As rendering 3D graphics is a computationally heavy process, we define the size of the memory required by our program when possible. The description `precision mediump float` in the fragment shader source informs the GPU of how much memory the shader operation demands.

Compiling

With the data for our application's shaders defined, we create and compile the shaders to link them to a program. The WebGL program is the container that carries our application's data through the pipeline. Yet, before we can create our shaders, we must first gain access to their source data from between the `<body>` tags in the HTML document. Write the following code in the JavaScript section of the *index.html* file beneath the error-checking of the `gl` variable:

```
// Create a variable to store the data for our vertex shader
const vsSource = document.querySelector("#vertex-data").text;

// Create a  variable to store the data from our fragment
   shader
const fsSource = document.querySelector("#fragment-data").
text;
```

As we did with the `<canvas>` element in our HTML, we store JavaScript references to our shader data through the DOM's `querySelector()` method. This time, however, we specify the content we'd like to pull from the element by appending the `.text` extension. The extension pulls the content of the shader source tags and saves it in the variables as `Strings`, a data type that defines an array of characters indexed by character, for example `['S','t','r','i','n','g']`.

```
// Compile the shaders into GLSL
const vertexShader = gl.createShader(gl.VERTEX_SHADER);
gl.shaderSource(vertexShader, vsSource);
gl.compileShader(vertexShader);
const fragmentShader = gl.createShader(gl.FRAGMENT_SHADER);
gl.shaderSource(fragmentShader, fsSource);
gl.compileShader(fragmentShader);
```

Now that we have the data for our shaders available in our JavaScript through the variables vsSource and fsSource, we can input them into the WebGL functions that create and compile the shaders. In compguter programming, compilation refers to the process of translating code from a human-readable format to one understood by a machine. Once compiled, a program is free to move beyond its source.

Linking

The vertex shader and fragment shader work cooperatively in a WebGL application. To that end, we must link them together through a single object.

```
// Create a carry-out container that will pass the shader
functions to the GPU
const program = gl.createProgram();
```

```
// Attach the shaders
gl.attachShader(program, vertexShader);
gl.attachShader(program, fragmentShader);
```

```
// Link the shaders
gl.linkProgram(program);
```

The process of compiling and linking programs is a common creation pattern for programs written in C and C++. For example, compiling and linking C++ programs for Windows applications result in an .exe file, which most developers recognize as Windows executable files. Once compiled into their own executables inside the program, the shaders move to the next phase of the graphics rendering pipeline.

Removing the gl.clearColor() and gl.clear() function calls from the JavaScript of our HTML document in the code editor, saving it, and reloading the browser shows that, again, our Web page is blank. Even though we have data, compiled shaders, and a program, we don't yet have a way for information to move from the browser to the screen.

Buffers

Buffers are programming objects that refer to memory allocated on a machine. They operate like queues at movie theaters or amusement parks; data comes in, waits, then moves out. In our WebGL application we will use buffer objects to save the state of our program during its passage to the GPU.

Setting Vertex Positions

First, we will need positions for where we wish to draw vertices on the screen. Below the creation of the WebGLRenderingContext in the JavaScript section of *index.html,* and above the code we added to create the shaders, add the following:

```
// Define the points in the scene
const coordinates = [
-0.7, 0.7,
-0.7, 0,
 0.7, 0,
];
```

Here, we create a JavaScript array called coordinates, which holds six elements. Though we've written them in the form of (x, y) coordinates, we could also define the array like this:

```
const coordinates = [-0.7, 0.7, -0.5, 0.0, 0.7, 0.0];
```

In either form, the data is the same—three pairs of coordinates. Since we have created the data for our vertices we need somewhere to store it:

```
// Create an empty buffer object to store the vertex points
const pointsBuffer = gl.createBuffer();
```

but our buffer object doesn't refer to any memory, yet; it is just an *idea* of a buffer object. That is, until we bind it:

```
// Connect the empty buffer object to the Gl context
gl.bindBuffer(gl.ARRAY_BUFFER, pointsBuffer);
```

The argument gl.ARRAY_BUFFER is a WebGL constant variable that specifies the type of buffer to use as the target for the buffer object we created. The value of the gl.ARRAY_BUFFER constant is a location of memory on the server to be sent in a data packet across the internet. It is, therefore, a binding point between our buffer, which holds vertex information and the WebGL context running in our browser tab.

```
// Load the vertices into the GL's connected buffer
gl.bufferData(gl.ARRAY_BUFFER, new Float32Array(coordinates),
gl.STATIC_DRAW);
```

Calling gl.bufferData() after binding our buffer sets the size of the data to send across the wire to the client's GPU to the size of the data in our buffer. The argument new Float32Array(coordinates) *casts* our array of 6 float elements into an array of 32-bit float values, a format optimized for mathematical operations on computers. The final argument, STATIC_DRAW, tells the GPU the data in our buffer will not be modified more than once and should be drawn to the browser's window. Storing the buffer data in its memory, the GPU saves time on future renders since the data remains the same.

Even though we've set the coordinates for our vertices and put them in a packet to be sent across the net, we aren't yet done writing the code in our application.

Connecting Shaders with Buffers

After we have linked both our vertex and fragment shader together in a program, we have an opportunity to funnel the coordinates we defined for our scene's vertices, defined in the coordinates array, into the attribute we set equal to the vertex shader's gl_Position property.

```
// Locate the attribute from the vertex shader source in the program
const pointsAttributeLocation = gl.getAttribLocation(program,
"vertex_points");
```

The WebGLRenderingContext's getAttribLocation() method queries the program for the index in which the GPU has saved the attribute we defined as "vertex_points" in our vertex-shader source.

```
// Connect the attribute to the points data currently in the
buffer object
gl.vertexAttribPointer(pointsAttributeLocation, 2, gl.FLOAT,
false, 0, 0);
```

Once we have the value of the index in which the GPU has stored the vertex-shader's "vertex_points" attribute, we can use it as part of a function to instruct the GPU how to parse the data in our vertex-shader executable, which we previously linked with the shader program. The arguments following the index value of the vertex attribute in the `gl.vertexAttribPointer()` method represent the number of coordinates per vertex, the data-type of the coordinates, whether or not to normalize the data, where in the coordinate array the GPU should begin its drawing, and how many indices to skip between coordinate pairs. For the sake of clarity, we can rewrite the previous function like this:

```
let size = 2;   // components per iteration (2 because just x,y
points)
let type = gl.FLOAT;    // data is 32bit floats
let normalize = false;
let stride = 0;    // don't skip indices between coordinate
pairs
let offset = 0; // start at beginning of buffer

gl.vertexAttribPointer(positionAttributeLocation, size, type,
normalize, stride, offset);
```

With the instruction set of how to read our vertex data set for the GPU, all that remains for us to do is activate the array buffer that contains our information:

```
    // Send the points data to the GPU
    gl.enableVertexAttribArray(pointsAttributeLocation);
```

Calling `gl.enableVertexAttribArray()` instructs the GPU to read the values from the array buffer specified by the `gl.vertexAttribPointer()` method. Finally, we notify the GPU it is time to render our image to the screen.

Drawing

We've already reviewed the first two steps of drawing to the WebGL canvas context. Here, we can reset the value of the clearColor vec4 to set the canvas to transparent and white.

```
// Clear the canvas
gl.clearColor(0, 0, 0, 0);

// Clear the color buffer for a fresh paint
gl.clear(gl.COLOR_BUFFER_BIT);
```

As we've already provided the GPU with the memory location of our shader information, we can call the WebGL drawArrays method to process the data as we've instructed.

```
// Draw the points on the screen
const mode = gl.TRIANGLES;
const first = 0;
const count = 3;
gl.drawArrays(mode, first, count);
```

The mode parameter instructs the GPU to connect three vertices to form a triangle; the first parameter instructs the GPU to begin reading the memory buffer from its start; and the count parameter instructs the GPU that our attribute buffer, as we defined in the vertexAttribPointer function, holds 3 counts of coordinate pairs of size 2. Save *index.html* in your code editor, activate your local server, and navigate to the page in a browser.

Do you see anything? If not, open your browser's Developer Tools by pressing CTRL + SHIFT + I in Edge and Chrome. The console will list any errors or notifications sent by our program. Here's what my browser's console reads:

```
WebGL: INVALID_OPERATION: drawArrays: no valid shader program
in use
```

If you've followed along with the code in this chapter, then you too should receive the same message. The solution is simple: we didn't instruct our application to use the program that we linked.

```
// Define the active program of the GL context
gl.linkProgram(program);
gl.useProgram(program);
```

Beneath the line in the JavaScript section of *index.html* where we linked our WebGL program, add the code that indicates which program the WebGLRenderingContext should use to retrieve our shader data.

Figure 2-3. *A low-resolution triangle projected onto a canvas context with the drawing buffer set to its default values*

Saving and loading the page should display a large, red, right triangle (Figure 2-3). The corners of the triangle correlate with the values we saved in the coordinates array in our JavaScript program. WebGL renders them into clip space on the canvas context we set, equal to the area of the browsing window in our CSS.

Resolution

The whole point of using the GPU to render graphics on the Web is to leverage the processor's power. Yet, a blurry, pixelated triangle seems far away from the high-definition promise of parallel execution. The reason our triangle appears blurry has nothing to do with the GPU, though. It has everything to do with a property of the canvas context called the drawing buffer, the default framebuffer for a WebGL context.

Enter the following in the JavaScript section of *index.html* immediately above the declaration of the coordinates array:

```
console.log(gl.drawingBufferWidth);
console.log(gl.drawingBufferHeight);
```

Saving and reloading the page will print the values of the width and height of the drawing buffer in the browser's console. The default values of the WebGLRenderingContext drawing buffer is 300px by 150px on my version of Microsoft Edge. Scaling the size of the canvas up without increasing the number of pixels within its borders results in poor resolution. To increase the resolution of the canvas, we can increase the area of the drawing buffer.

```
<canvas id="c" width="1216" height="1334"></canvas>
```

Redefine the dimensions of the <canvas> element in the HTML <body> tag of *index.html*. While setting the dimensions of the canvas in CSS alters the size of the canvas, we increase the size of the canvas' drawing buffer by defining its dimensions directly in the <canvas> tag.

Figure 2-4. *A high-resolution triangle drawn to a canvas context with a drawing buffer area set in HTML*

Saving and reloading the scene should present a more sharply rendered triangle in the browser (Figure 2-4). The Oculus Quest presents content through its headset on two 1600×1440 pixel OLED screens that run at 72 frames per second. By default, Quest apps render to 1216×1334 pixel eye textures, the framebuffer for each eye. That should give you an idea of how incredibly efficient the communication between hardware and WebGL has become.

Modes of Drawing

Since we've done so much work setting up our application to draw to the canvas in the browser, let's perform a final task before closing the chapter. So far we have rendered three vertices to the canvas, which the GPU connected to form a triangle. What happens if we add a fourth vertex?

```
// Define the points in the scene
const coordinates = [
-0.7, 0.7,
-0.7, 0,
 0.7, 0,
 0.7, 0.7
];
```

Add the coordinate pair (0.7, 0.7) to the last two indices of the coordinates array. Save and reload the page.

Nothing happened. Recall that in the instruction we sent to the GPU through the drawArrays() call, we set the count parameter to 3. However, after adding another coordinate pair to our coordinates array, we now have 4 coordinates instead of 3. Change the value of count to 4.

```
// Draw the points on the screen
const mode = gl.TRIANGLE_STRIP;
const first = 0;
const count = 4;
gl.drawArrays(mode, first, count);
```

Also change the value of the mode parameter from gl.TRIANGLES to gl.TRIANGLE_STRIP. Save and reload the scene.

Figure 2-5. *Four vertices drawn to the canvas context with the drawing mode parameter set to* triangle_strip

What the heck is going on? Well, WebGL includes several different modes with which it can draw to the browser's canvas. Whereas gl.TRIANGLE connected 3 points to form a triangle, gl.TRIANGLE_STRIP connects each additional point to its two predecessors to form a strip of connected triangles (Figure 2-5). Changing the mode parameter to gl.LINE_LOOP connects each vertex with a line and connects the last to the first, forming the outline of a rectangle (Figure 2-6).

Figure 2-6. *Four vertices drawn to the canvas context with the drawing mode parameter set to* `line_loop`

To create a solid box from two triangles, we can change the order of how the GPU reads the vertices from the buffer.

```
const coordinates = [
-0.7, 0.7,
 0.7, 0.7,
-0.7, 0,
 0.7, 0,
];
```

Rearranging the vertices in the coordinates array by their location, moving clockwise around the plane beginning with the top-left, allows the GPU to complete a square (Figure 2-7). Reset the mode of the `drawArrays` function to `gl.TRIANGLE_STRIP`, save, and reload the page.

Figure 2-7. *Four vertices drawn to the canvas context with the drawing mode set to* `triangle_strip` *and the vertices defined in sequential order clockwise from left*

Now, that's much better.

Summary

By completing Exercise 1 you have gone through the process of creating the state of a WebGL application, defining its behavior, and drawing its content to the canvas context of a browser. The steps you followed to create the application make up the core of the WebGL rendering process. In the next chapter we will address an important component of the WebGL API that will take our application to another dimension.

Key takeaways include:

- A WebGL application requires a WebGLRenderingContext.

- A WebGL context extends the functionality of the Canvas API.

- Vertex shaders define how the GPU draws and connects points on the screen.

- A fragment shader defines the color the GPU applies to a pixel on a screen.

- Attributes define the data in a vertex shader's source.

- WebGL stores data in buffers before passing it from target to source.

- A WebGL program is a container for shaders and their data.

- A draw command instructs the GPU on what to render to the screen and how.

CHAPTER 3

Toward the Third Dimension in WebGL

We completed the previous chapter with a red rectangle painted into the window of a Web browser. The process to make the rectangle included the following steps: setting up data inside a vertex and fragment shader; storing the information in buffers; and commanding the WebGL application to execute its drawing instructions. If these steps make up the state and behavior of a WebGL program that rasterizes 2D content, and every WebGL program is a machine that operates on state, then how can we use what we have already created to add a third dimension to our scene?

The following exercise and its three parts build upon the lessons of the last. Because graphics specifications like OpenGL implement the structure of a pipeline to render polygons made of vertices, we, as developers, don't have much to do more than create the framework for the plumbing and toss in our coordinates. As we've already met the principle players in the pipeline, like the vertex array, the buffer, the attribute pointer, and the shader, for example, we are well on our way to creating three-dimensional content using only WebGL in the browser. Here, we will expand the capacity of our pipeline to accommodate more vertices, more coordinates, and more colors in our scene; we will increase the amount of data in our pipeline to increase the dimensions of its state.

© Rakesh Baruah 2021
R. Baruah, *AR and VR Using the WebXR API*,
https://doi.org/10.1007/978-1-4842-6318-1_3

In this chapter you will learn:

- How to write JavaScript separate from an HTML file

- How to draw multiple shapes in a WebGL context

- How to add color values to specific vertices

- The meaning and application of varying qualifiers in shader programs

- The meaning of the depth buffer and its application to rendering

- The differing drawing modes available in WebGL

The ABCs of XYZ

A Cartesian coordinate plane defines its first two dimensions with x and y axes. By adding a z-axis (perpendicular, or orthogonal) to the first two, we introduce a third dimension to our scene (Figure 3-1).

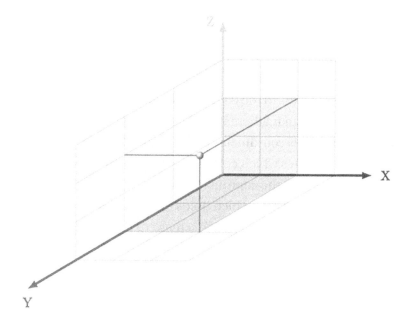

Figure 3-1. *Adding a z-axis to a Cartesian coordinate plane creates a third dimension*

Though 3D software packages use different orientations of their axes, for our purposes we can imagine an x-axis increasing in value to its right, a y-axis increasing in value toward the sky, and the z-axis increasing in value as it moves outward from our chest. In the following exercise we will, among other things, amend the code from the previous chapter with a z-coordinate to render a third dimension.

Exercise 2, Part 1: Painting in the Third Dimension

To begin, you can work from the documents you saved from the previous chapter, download the source code from the course's GitHub repository, or begin from scratch. Here, I will begin from scratch to reinforce the steps of building the WebGL pipeline.

The WebGL Pipeline

The WebGL pipeline (Figure 3-2) collects coordinates of points in 3D space, called vertices, and stores them in data structures called buffers. The buffers act as couriers to the GPU of a client device, where the vertex coordinates pass through mathematical functions called shaders. The vertex shader transposes coordinates into clip space, while the fragment, or pixel, shader calculates which color to paint each pixel. Then, the WebGL pipeline transfers the coordinates of each vertex and color value for each pixel to a framebuffer, which holds the contents of the image before the GPU renders it to the client's screen.

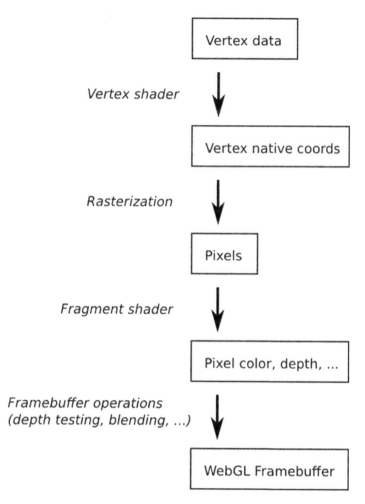

Figure 3-2. *The WebGL pipeline accepts vertex coordinates as inputs. After passing through a collection of buffers and mathematical functions, called shaders, the coordinates arrive at a framebuffer where they wait to be rendered to a screen*

In Part 1 of this exercise you will:

- Outline the phases of the WebGL pipeline in code

- Separate JavaScript from HTML syntax in a JavaScript file

- Increase the number of vertices stored in a WebGL buffer

- Add a z-coordinate value for a vertex

- Define shader source code using JavaScript template literals

- Change the mode of the WebGL Draw method

Setup

1. Create a new index.html document in VS Code by entering an exclamation point and then pressing Enter.

```
<!DOCTYPE html>
<html lang="en">
<head>
    <meta charset="UTF-8">
    <meta name="viewport" content="width=device-width,
    initial-scale=1.0">
    <title>Document</title>
</head>
<body>

</body>
</html>
```

2. Add a canvas element with an id and CSS styles defining the canvas layout.

```
<html lang="en">
<head>
    <meta charset="UTF-8">
```

```
<meta name="viewport" content="width=device-width,
initial-scale=1.0">
<title>WebGL Lesson 2: third Dimension</title>
<style>
    canvas {
        width: 100vw;
        height: 100vh;
    }
</style>
</head>
<body>
    <canvas id="c" width=1920 height=1080></canvas>
</body>
</html>
```

3. Create a new file and save it as index.js. Above the
    closing HTML tag in index.html add a script tag
    pointing to the JavaScript file.

```
<body>
    <canvas id="c" width=1920 height=1080></canvas>
</body>
<script src="index.js"></script>
</html>
```

The src attribute on the script tag points to the relative file path of your
JS file. For this exercise, make sure your index.html and JS file live in the
same folder, at the same level. Later in the course we will address creating
subfolders inside directories.

A Separation of Concerns

1. In `index.js` define a main function and add the
   following template headings. Alternatively, you can
   download the `webGLtemplate.js` template from the
   lesson files in the course GitHub repository.

```
function main() {
    /*========= Create a WebGL Context =========*/

    /*========= Define and Store the Geometry
    =========*/

    /*====== Define front-face vertices ======*/
    /*====== Define front-face buffer ======*/

    /*========= Shaders =========*/

    /*====== Define shader source ======*/
    /*====== Create shaders ======*/
    /*====== Compile shaders ======*/
    /*====== Create shader program ======*/
    /*====== Link shader program ======*/

    /*====== Connect the attribute with the vertex shader
    ======*/

    /*========= Drawing ========= */

    /*====== Draw the points to the screen ======*/

}
```

A WebGL program operates as a state machine. Data describing
the position and color of vertices, for example, update over time. The
appearance of a WebGL scene, therefore, is a function of its appearance
in the frame prior. In this exercise we will change the input data to our
shaders to affect the state of the WebGL context over time.

Before we address altering the input into our WebGL pipeline, let's attend to a bit of housekeeping first. As transitions over time introduce complexity to an application, we separate our JavaScript code from the HTML document to simplify the architecture. The act of compartmentalizing code files in a project based on their domain of execution is called a Separation of Concerns. As HTML is a markup language primarily responsible for the appearance of our page, the philosophy of a Separation of Concerns suggests we write the code to manage the behavior of our page in another file.

An Array of Possibilities

With the logic of our JavaScript separated from the presentational syntax of our HTML document, we can continue with our exercise.

1. We create a WebGL context as we did before:

    ```
    /*========== Create a WebGL Context ==========*/
    const canvas = document.querySelector("#c");
    const gl = canvas.getContext('webgl');
    if (!gl) {
        console.log('WebGL unavailable');
    } else {
        console.log('WebGL is good to go');
    }
    ```

2. While in the previous exercise we created a square by defining four vertices in a 2-dimensional plane, in this exercise we will define six vertices: three for each triangle that together form a square. We will give each vertex a third coordinate to define its position along the z-axis.

```
/*========== Define and Store the Geometry ==========*/
const firstSquare = [
    // front face
    -0.3 , -0.3, -0.3,
     0.3, -0.3, -0.3,
     0.3, 0.3, -0.3,

    -0.3, -0.3, -0.3,
    -0.3, 0.3, -0.3,
     0.3, 0.3, -0.3,
];
```

We use values between -1 and 1 to define the locations of the vertices because the WebGLRenderingContext interprets the coordinates of the canvas between -1 and 1.[1] These coordinates lie in clip space as opposed to world space, a concept we will discuss in more detail in a following chapter on the view matrix.

3. The array of points we defined becomes the new state of our scene WebGL will render. The initialization of the attribute buffer object we defined in the last exercise remains the same, though we change the name of the vertex array we bind to the buffer.

---

[1]Clip space coordinates normalize the scales of x and y axes between -1 and 1. The z-axis, however, extends negatively from the camera beginning at 0. Normalized device coordinates (NDCs), on the other hand, constrain all three axes between -1 and 1. The WebGL pipeline normalizes screen coordinates to standardize experiences across dimensions of all screens.

```
// buffer
const origBuffer = gl.createBuffer();
gl.bindBuffer(gl.ARRAY_BUFFER, origBuffer);
gl.bufferData(gl.ARRAY_BUFFER, new Float32Array
(firstSquare), gl.STATIC_DRAW);
```

As we are writing our JS and GLSL code in a file separate from our HTML, we will also define our shader source differently than we did previously.

Literally Speaking

Because our index.js file is a JavaScript file, a Web browser will interpret its content as JS. Here, a type attribute indicating text that is "not-javascript" won't work. However, since we know that WebGL vertex and fragment shaders accept strings as input, we can use template literals to bound the GLSL shader source code in our script. In JS, template literals, represented by the backtick character, allow for multiline strings and embedded expressions.

1. Using the backtick character, which is located to the left of the number 1 on the horizontal number pad on most US keyboards, store the shader source code in target variables.

```
const vsSource = `
    attribute vec4 aPosition;

    void main() {
        gl_Position = aPosition;
    }
`;

const fsSource = `
    void main() {
```

```
        gl_FragColor = vec4(1, 0, 0, 1);
    }
`;
```

2. Code to create, compile, and link the vertex and
   fragment shaders to a new program remains as it
   was in the previous exercise.

```
//create shaders
const vertexShader = gl.createShader(gl.VERTEX_SHADER);
const fragmentShader = gl.createShader(gl.FRAGMENT_
SHADER);
gl.shaderSource(vertexShader, vsSource);
gl.shaderSource(fragmentShader, fsSource);

// compile shaders
gl.compileShader(vertexShader);
gl.compileShader(fragmentShader);

// create program
const program = gl.createProgram();
gl.attachShader(program, vertexShader);
gl.attachShader(program, fragmentShader);

// link program
gl.linkProgram(program);
gl.useProgram(program);
```

Move the Pointer

To connect the program's attribute with the pipeline, we only have to
change one parameter from the previous lesson's code.

1. As we've added a z-coordinate to our `firstSquare`
    coordinate array, we change the parameter from 2 to 3.

    ```
    /*========= Connect the attribute with the vertex
    shader =========*/
    const posAttribLocation = gl.getAttribLocation(program,
    "aPosition");
    gl.bindBuffer(gl.ARRAY_BUFFER, origBuffer);
    gl.vertexAttribPointer(posAttribLocation, 3, gl.FLOAT,
    false, 0, 0);
    gl.enableVertexAttribArray(posAttribLocation);
    ```

The second argument of the `gl.vertexAttribPointer()` function asks
for the number of coordinates to count for each vertex.

Calling the Drawing Mode

As suggested by its name, the draw method flushes our framebuffer from
the pipeline to the client's screen. However, before sending our image on
its way, let's experiment with changing some of the method's arguments.

1. Before writing the draw call for the main function,
    we reset the color of the WebGL context to an
    opaque white. For this exercise, we will reset the
    drawing mode of the `gl.drawArrays()` method to
    `gl.TRIANGLES`.

    ```
    /*========= Drawing ========= */
    gl.clearColor(1, 1, 1, 1);
    gl.clear(gl.COLOR_BUFFER_BIT);
    // Draw the points on the screen
    const mode = gl.TRIANGLES;
    const first = 0;
    const count = 6;
    ```

```
    gl.drawArrays(mode, first, count);
} // be sure to close the main function with a curly brace.
```

We update the count variable from 4 to 6 because
we do not want our program to assume our triangles
share vertices.

2. At the top of the index.js file, before the declaration
   of the main function, *call* the main function by typing:[2]

```
main();
function main() {...
```

A Web browser compiles JS code as it's received
from the server. Calling the main() function before
or after its declaration makes no difference, as the
browser has already stored the function's reference
prior to executing any script. Later in the course
we discuss ES modules in JavaScript, which offer a
different kind of functionality.

3. Save both the index.html and index.js files in VS
   Code, launch your local Web server, and load the
   HTML page. You should see a red square/rectangle
   (depending on your browser's dimensions) in the
   center of your browser's canvas (Figure 3-3).

---

[2]An alternative approach is to call the main() function as an IIFE, an immediately
invoked function expression. We will discuss patterns such as this in a later
chapter on JavaScript modules.

Figure 3-3. *A red square drawn by the GPU using the TRIANGLES mode in WebGL*

Changing the mode variable in index.js to `gl.LINE_LOOP` from `gl.TRIANGLES` demonstrates how WebGL connected the six vertices we provided into two triangles that form a square (Figure 3-4).

Figure 3-4. *A square rendered by the GPU with the WebGL drawing mode set to LINE_LOOP*

As computer graphics is a quest for the smallest use of memory, asking the GPU to connect two extraneous vertices to form a square is not common practice at all. However, for this exercise it is more important to understand the order in which WebGL renders multiple shapes rather than individual vertices.

Even though we added a third coordinate to the array that defined the positions of our square's coordinates, our image still only appears in two dimensions. In Part 2 of this exercise we will add a second square with a different value for its vertices' z-coordinate. Perhaps that will better illustrate the 3D capabilities of WebGL. Before we continue, though, let us review what we learned in Part 1.

In Part 1 of this exercise you:

- Separated JavaScript code from HTML syntax in a separate JS file

- Expanded the vertex array of the square's face to include a z-coordinate for each vertex

- Increased the size of the buffer object to accommodate the additional coordinates in the array

- Incremented the stride of the WebGL attribute pointer to include the z-coordinate added to the array

- Embedded GLSL code in JavaScript using template literals

- Changed the mode of the WebGL draw command

Exercise 2, Part 2: Squares Squared

In Part 2 of this exercise we will explore how we can better achieve the illusion of 3-dimensional depth in our WebGL scene. We will build on what we created in Part 1 by drawing a second square in the browser. We will also manipulate the values passed into the fragment shader of the WebGL pipeline to determine how the colors of our shapes impact the appearance of overlapping bodies.

In Part 2 of this exercise you will:

- Add the coordinates of a second square's vertices to the vertex array from Part 1

- Offset the plane shared by shapes by altering the shapes' z-coordinates

- Amend the WebGL draw command to draw two squares instead of one

- Add an attribute to the vertex shader to hold color data stored in a vector

- Create another buffer object to hold the data from the color attribute

- Connect the color buffer to the WebGL shader program through a second binding point

- Use the WebGL "varying" qualifier in both the vertex and fragment shader source to create a color gradient between rendered vertices

Z-Town

We begin Part 2 as the WebGL pipeline begins, with the vertices of our shape. Referring to the position coordinates of our first square in Part 1, you'll notice the value of our third coordinate for each vertex:

```
const firstSquare = [
    // front face
    -0.3 , -0.3, -0.3,
     0.3, -0.3, -0.3,
     0.3, 0.3, -0.3,
```

```
    -0.3, -0.3, -0.3,
    -0.3, 0.3, -0.3,
     0.3, 0.3, -0.3,
];
```

The value -0.3 for the z-coordinate places the square closer to our point of view than the origin. Yet, without a frame of reference, the square appears to have no depth at all. Let's address this by adding a second square to our scene *behind* the first.

1. In the same index.js file from Part 1, amend the coordinates of the firstSquare array with the following values:

```
/*========== Define and Store the Geometry ==========*/

const squares = [
    // front face
    -0.3 , -0.3, -0.3,
     0.3, -0.3, -0.3,
     0.3, 0.3, -0.3,

    -0.3, -0.3, -0.3,
    -0.3, 0.3, -0.3,
     0.3, 0.3, -0.3,

    // back face
    -0.2, -0.2, 0.3,
    0.4, -0.2, 0.3,
    0.4, 0.4, 0.3,

    -0.2, -0.2, 0.3,
    -0.2, 0.4, 0.3,
    0.4, 0.4, 0.3,
];
```

In addition to offsetting the x and y coordinates by 0.1, we've also changed the z-coordinate from -0.3 to 0.3. Because the z-axis moves away from our point of view as its value increases, a positive z value will place a coordinate behind one with a negative value, from our frame of reference.

2. In the same code block where we created the buffer object, change the target variable of the coordinates array from firstSquare to squares. Replace the value of the gl.bufferData method from firstSquare to squares, too.

```
gl.bufferData(gl.ARRAY_BUFFER, new
Float32Array(squares), gl.STATIC_DRAW);
```

Finally, because we have added 6 more vertices to our buffer data, we must instruct the GPU to draw 12 vertices, or four triangles, instead of only 6.

3. Change the count variable from 6 to 12...

```
const mode = gl.TRIANGLES;
const first = 0;
const count = 12;
gl.drawArrays(mode, first, count);
```

Save the index.js file and reload the Web page in your browser.

You should see two red squares as in Figure 3-5. Because the squares share the same color, it's difficult to tell which sits in front of the other. To address this, let's instruct our WebGL program to apply the color blue to the square with the positive z-coordinates.

Figure 3-5. *Two red squares with different values for their vertices'*
z-coordinates rendered to the screen

A Second Color

To add a second color to our fragment shader, we first must amend our
shader source data.

```
// shaders
const vsSource = `
    attribute vec4 aPosition;
    attribute vec4 aVertexColor;

    varying lowp vec4 vColor;

    void main() {
        gl_Position = aPosition;
        vColor = aVertexColor;
    }
`;

const fsSource = `
    varying lowp vec4 vColor;
```

```
    void main() {
        gl_FragColor = vColor;
    }
`;
```

1. Add a second attribute to the vertex shader
    source code. Define it as a Vector4 with the name
    aVertexColor. Then, add a varying qualifier to
    the vertex shader source code of type lowp vec4
    and name it vColor. Add the same qualifier to the
    fragment shader and set the target variable gl_
    FragColor to the value of the varying called vColor.

    Here, again, vec4 informs the compiler to expect
    a vector with four indices, each representing a
    value of r, g, b, and alpha, or opacity. The keyword
    lowp informs the compiler to reserve just enough
    memory to hold a low-precision float value. While
    an attribute qualifier defines data unique to the
    vertex shader, a varying qualifier applies to a
    fragment shader too. Why a varying qualifier has the
    name it does will become apparent before the end
    of this exercise.

2. Because we've added a second attribute to the
    vertex shader, we have to create another buffer to
    hold the data to pass from the server to the client.
    Above the shaders heading in index.js, add the
    following JS code:

```
const colorBuffer = gl.createBuffer();
gl.bindBuffer(gl.ARRAY_BUFFER, colorBuffer);
gl.bufferData(gl.ARRAY_BUFFER, new
Float32Array(squareColors), gl.STATIC_DRAW);
```

Just as we did with the buffer object that holds the coordinates of our vertices, we bind the buffer holding our program's color information to the WebGL context through a gl.ARRAY_BUFFER binding point.

Notice the value of the parameter we cast as a new Float32Array in the parentheses following the gl.bufferData method call. It's a variable called squareColors, but where in our program do we have an object called squareColors? We don't! Yet, since the buffer holding our color data is the same type of buffer holding our coordinate data, we can package the information in a similarly structured array.

3. Between the declarations of the two buffers, origBuffer and colorBuffer, add a declaration for an array called squareColors. Fill it with the following values:

```
const squareColors = [
    0.0,  0.0,  1.0,  1.0,
    0.0,  0.0,  1.0,  1.0,
    0.0,  0.0,  1.0,  1.0,
    0.0,  0.0,  1.0,  1.0,
    0.0,  0.0,  1.0,  1.0,
    0.0,  0.0,  1.0,  1.0,

    1.0,  0.0,  0.0,  1.0,
    1.0,  0.0,  0.0,  1.0,
    1.0,  0.0,  0.0,  1.0,
```

```
    1.0,   0.0,   0.0,   1.0,
    1.0,   0.0,   0.0,   1.0,
    1.0,   0.0,   0.0,   1.0,
];
```

Recall that we defined a vec4 attribute in our vertex
shader source as aVertexColor. In the main()
method of the vertex shader source code we saved
whatever value the attribute holds to the vec4
varying variable vColor. As attributes do not move
past the vertex shader in the WebGL pipeline, the
varying variable vColor carries the data stored in
the aVertexColor attribute to the fragment shader.
Defining a color attribute in the vertex shader
and passing it to the fragment shader as a varying
qualifier connects each rgba vector4 color value
with a vertex in our squares array. As each row in
the array squareColors defines the color value of a
vertex, the fragment shader varies the color between
vertices along a gradient. That is why the varying
qualifier has the name it does, and we will see it in
action soon.

But first, we have to point the program connected
to our WebGL context to the addresses in memory
where we have stored the color data of our scene.

4. Beneath the code activating the buffer that holds
    our vertex data, create a target variable for the
    aVertexColor attribute address. Then bind the
    buffer to the gl program and turn it on:

```
/*========== Connect the attribute with the vertex
shader ==========*/
const posAttribLocation = gl.getAttribLocation
(program, "aPosition");
gl.vertexAttribPointer(posAttribLocation, 3, gl.FLOAT,
false, 0, 0);
gl.enableVertexAttribArray(posAttribLocation);

const colorAttribLocation =
gl.getAttribLocation(program, "aVertexColor");
gl.bindBuffer(gl.ARRAY_BUFFER, colorBuffer);
gl.vertexAttribPointer(colorAttribLocation, 4,
gl.FLOAT, false, 0, 0);
gl.enableVertexAttribArray(colorAttribLocation);
```

Note the difference between the parameters of
the two gl.vertexAttribPointer methods. The
method that creates a pointer to the memory
location of our squares array in the aPosition
attribute defines the size argument with the value 3.
The argument informs the GPU that each vertex in
our program has 3 coordinates. On the other hand,
because 4 values define the color of each vertex in
the squareColors array, we pass the value 4 as the
size argument for the function that creates a pointer
to the aVertexColor attribute.

5. As we've introduced more data to our application,
   we've also introduced more complexity. To better
   handle any errors that may emerge during the
   compilation of our program, let's add some error
   handling to the methods responsible for compiling
   our shaders.

```
// compile shaders
gl.compileShader(vertexShader);
if (!gl.getShaderParameter(vertexShader, gl.COMPILE_
STATUS)) {
    alert('An error occurred compiling the shaders: '
    + gl.getShaderInfoLog(vertexShader));
    gl.deleteShader(vertexShader);
    return null;
  }
gl.compileShader(fragmentShader);
if (!gl.getShaderParameter(fragmentShader, gl.COMPILE_
STATUS)) {
    alert('An error occurred compiling the shaders: '
    + gl.getShaderInfoLog(fragmentShader));
    gl.deleteShader(fragmentShader);
    return null;
  }
```

If you're genuinely interested in the details of the code to handle errors during the compilation of shaders, then please refer to the OpenGL ES specification or the documentation for the WebGL API on the Mozilla Developer's Network website. It's sufficient for our purpose to know that if an error occurs in our program, the WebGL context provides methods to access details explaining the problem.

6. Finally, let's amend our Draw call to reflect the changes we've made to the state and behavior of our program. Add the following three methods beneath the gl.clearColor() method call:

```
gl.enable(gl.DEPTH_TEST);
gl.depthFunc(gl.LEQUAL);
gl.clear(gl.COLOR_BUFFER_BIT | gl.DEPTH_BUFFER_BIT);
```

Enabling DEPTH_TEST on the gl context allows the
GPU to evaluate the order of vertices in our scene
along the z-axis. Adding gl.DEPTH_BUFFER_BIT to
the gl.clear() method parameters instructs the
GPU to reset the color and depth data to default
values prior to drawing the scene.

7.   Save the file index.js and reload the Web page in
your Web browser.

Depending on the scale of your browser window, you should see either
two squares or two rectangles, one blue and the other red, as in Figure 3-6.
As the first six rows of the squareColors array define the color blue for the
first six rows of the squares array, the square closest to us, with the negative
z-coordinates, appears in front of the red square.

Figure 3-6. *Rendering the pixels in the rectangle with the higher
z-coordinate value in blue demonstrates the order of the draw call's
executions*

Changing some of the RGBA values of the squareColors array will
demonstrate how the fragment shader varies the color of the canvas
between vertices (Figure 3-7).

Figure 3-7. *The varying qualifier in the vertex shader instructs the fragment shader to interpolate the color values between vertices into a gradient*

Of course, one colored plane atop another does not create a convincingly 3-dimensional scene. In Part 3 of this exercise we'll add a third plane to our scene, one that creates a bridge connecting the foreground to the back. Perhaps the addition of a "top" to create a 3-sided cube will better convey the depth of our scene.

Exercise 2, Part 3: Three Sides for Three Dimensions

In the previous two parts of this exercise, we demonstrated that our WebGL application is a state machine. We provide input to the shaders of our program and they render the appearance of our scene, its state, to our browser's screen. Because we haven't yet introduced time into our program, our state has been static. Yet, the value a state machine provides is a constant pipeline regardless of the input. In other words, we've done all the hard work!

More Shapes, More Vertices, More Coordinates

To add a third square to our scene, we simply add vertices and their colors
to the buffers in our code.

1. Add the following six vertices to the end of the
   squares array:

   ```
   // top face
   -0.3, 0.3, -0.3,
    0.3, 0.3, -0.3,
   -0.2, 0.4,  0.3,

    0.4, 0.4,  0.3,
    0.3, 0.3, -0.3,
   -0.2, 0.4,  0.3,
   ];
   ```

2. Add the following six rows of vec4 values to the
   bottom of the squareColors array:

   ```
   ...
   0.0,  1.0,  0.0,  1.0,
   0.0,  1.0,  0.0,  1.0,
   0.0,  1.0,  0.0,  1.0,
   0.0,  1.0,  0.0,  1.0,
   0.0,  1.0,  0.0,  1.0,
   0.0,  1.0,  0.0,  1.0,
   ];
   ```

3. Finally, update the value of the count variable in the
   gl.drawArrays() method from 12 to 18, as we've
   added 6 more vertices to our squares array.

```
...
   const mode = gl.TRIANGLES;
   const first = 0;
   const count = 18;
   gl.drawArrays(mode, first, count);
```

4. Save the JS file and reload the HTML page in your
    browser.

You should see a cube with three-sides: one blue, one green, and
one red (Figure 3-8). Though the cube is 3D, as it has different values
along the z-axis, it doesn't provide the illusion of depth. Here, depending
on your mood, we encounter either a feature or bug of WebGL. Unlike
other 3D libraries, WebGL does not provide built-in, ready-made tools to
view a scene with depth. Other 3D libraries provide the feature of depth
perception through a virtual camera, which can create perspective, the
phenomenon of parallel lines appearing to converge toward a vanishing
point in the distance.

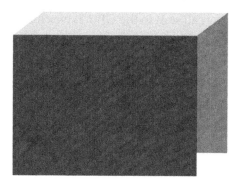

Figure 3-8. *A three-sided cube rendered through the declaration of*
vertices

Math Magic

However, the illusion of perspective is just that—an illusion. There's nothing inherently magical to a virtual camera that distorts parallel lines. In fact, it's not magical at all; it's linear algebra, and we can recreate the effect of perspective in our scene by applying rudimentary matrix math to our vertices with WebGL. In the next chapter we will complete our introductory foray into WebGL by introducing the roles played by matrix multiplication in 3D computer graphics.

Summary

In this chapter we explored how to edit an image rendered to a WebGL context. We learned that by adding x and y coordinates to a vertex array and expanding the size of its buffer, we can increase the number and complexity of shapes in our scene. The mechanics of the WebGL pipeline also became clearer to us, as we incremented the value of the indices between each vertex in an attribute pointer array. The WebGL pipeline is, after all, simply a state machine: a program that accepts vertices and vectors as input, which it modifies with each draw call sent to the GPU. If we change the data sent into the WebGL pipeline, then we can change the appearance of our scene.

In addition to more vertices, we also sent two new types of information through our pipeline. The first was, literally, a new dimension. By setting the value of a z-coordinate in the vertex array, buffer, and shader, we gave the GPU information it needed to schedule the order of appearance of our shapes. The second was a vector of color values, which we included in our vertex and fragment shaders with the "varying" qualifier. Among the lessons learned was that the WebGL pipeline sees only data. Position, orientation, size, and even color are but floating point numbers to the calculating cores running the operations in our program. As artists and developers, we arrange the information of our scenes in WebGL; its pipeline, a state machine, renders it into being.

Key takeaways of this chapter include:

- How to include JavaScript in an HTML document from a separate file

- How to draw multiple shapes to a canvas by adding vertices to an array

- How to apply color values to specific vertices through the use of attributes in the vertex shader

- How a fragment shader uses varyings to interpolate color between vertices

- How to order the drawing of vertices with different z-coordinates

- How to affect the appearance of vertices through different drawing modes in WebGL

CHAPTER 4

Matrices, Transformations, and Perspective in WebGL

Until now in our journey along the WebGL pipeline, we have conveniently avoided any talk of linear algebra. While the subject used to give my heart palpitations too, I've learned over time that programming 3D graphics provides a helpful, visual tool for the understanding of what linear algebra is. In short, linear algebra is the manipulation of coordinate space in ways that: 1) keep the xyz origin at (0, 0, 0); and 2) keep parallel lines parallel.[1] Of course there are many more complicated applications of linear algebra such as in neural networks and quantum physics. However, I have found for an intuitive understanding of the role linear algebra plays in 3D computer graphics, the two fundamental features I've presented suffice. By maintaining the location of the origin in three dimensions and the parallel nature of parallel lines, linear algebra helps XR developers compute

---

[1] For an elegant, thorough introduction to linear algebra, watch the "Essence of Linear Algebra" video by the YouTube creator 3 Blue 1 Brown.

© Rakesh Baruah 2021
R. Baruah, *AR and VR Using the WebXR API*,
https://doi.org/10.1007/978-1-4842-6318-1_4

transformations of shapes in context and without unintended distortion. Linear algebra maps the three dimensions of our world onto the two dimensions of our screens, and in concert with graphics hardware it does so ridiculously fast.

In this chapter you will learn:

- How APIs like WebGL use matrix multiplication to move vertices on a screen

- How to translate, scale, and rotate vertices with a single transformation matrix

- How to conveniently execute matrix multiplication in JavaScript

- The shortcomings of Euler angles and the strengths offered by quaternions

- Why GPUs perform so well with matrix math

- How to animate rotation of a an object in a WebGL program using JavaScript

- How to recreate 3D perspective on a 2D plane with a matrix

A Box of Maps

To begin, we'll start with an analogy.

What if I told you I want a cheeseburger? What if I then told you I wanted a milkshake? And then a video game, a sweater, and a plate of nachos? First, you'd probably say you don't know me like that. Sure, but for the sake of this example, will you just agree?

Great. So, you have the list of items I want. Another complication, however, is that I want you to get these things from only my favorite stores. Since you don't know me like that, I will give you a collection of lists that outline the driving directions from my house to each destination. You will receive a stack of papers (Figure 4-1). Page 1 will explain how to get from my house to the cheeseburger stand; page 2 will explain how to get from my house to a secret milkshake spot across town; page 3 will have directions from my house to the electronics store that sells video games; and so on. Got it? Good! See you later.

Figure 4-1. *A stack of maps I provide to help you with the errands I've assigned in the analogy that begins this chapter*

You're back so soon. What happened?

If you actually indulged my demands in real life, you'd likely realize after picking up my burger that you don't have driving directions from the burger stand to the milkshake spot. None of the directions I gave you explain how to move between the locations; only from my house to a single, specific building. The help I've offered you isn't really helpful at all.

Okay, I have a better idea. Here are pages that have driving directions between every location I want you to visit in the order I made the request (Figure 4-2). The list begins with directions from my house to the burger stand; then it instructs you how to drive from the burger stand to the milkshake spot, to the electronics store, and so on. Now, off you go; I'll see you in a bit.

Figure 4-2. *Illustrations of maps I provide to help you navigate the errands I assign in the analogy that opens this chapter*

You're back again? What happened this time?

Well, it turns out a construction crew has dug up the road I listed as the best route from the burger stand to the milkshake spot. Without an alternate route, you had no choice but to return with just my burger. But I can't eat a cheeseburger without a milkshake! You must go back out there or I am going to starve. To help you on your way, here is a map with the routes between each stop highlighted (Figure 4-3). If you encounter any further road blocks, then use the map to make your own way. Call if you have any trouble. I'll see you soon.

Figure 4-3. *An illustration of a complete map I provide to help you complete the errands assigned in this chapter's analogy. A concatenated transformation matrix serves as such a map for vertices in a 3D scene*

Matrices function like maps in 3D graphics. Their row and column structure provides a convenient, standardized model to communicate information inside a 3D graphics program, like one written with the WebGL API. An example of the information a matrix can hold and provide in a program is movement. In a way, a matrix is a kind of map for the vertices in our scenes to follow.

What You May Have Missed in Algebra 2

In the context of 3D graphics and transformations, a matrix is a data structure that holds the values that *describe* the movement we'd like our vertices to perform. A matrix can quite literally *transform* a shape's position, size, and/or orientation (Figure 4-4): processes known as translation, scaling, and rotation, respectively.

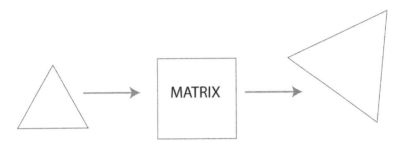

Figure 4-4. *A matrix operates as a function that transforms the position, size, and/or orientation of a set of vertices on a coordinate plane*

Translation

Translation of vertices describes their movement without reorientation. Let's say we want to move a triangle on our screen a few pixels to the right. Instead of creating a new array of vertices to define the location of the translation coordinates, we can add the values of our original coordinates to an amount that matches the distance our triangle will move.

If the triangle will retain its shape and dimensions after its move, then we add the coordinates of each vertex to the same distance values. For example, we add each value of x to the same number and each value of y to the same number. The output is a facsimile of the original triangle translated x values to the right and y values up, if both Δx and Δy are positive (Figure 4-5). We can codify the distance and direction we'd like the triangle to move by creating a translation matrix and multiplying it by a vector of the x, y, and z coordinates for each vertex in our scene (Figure 4-6).

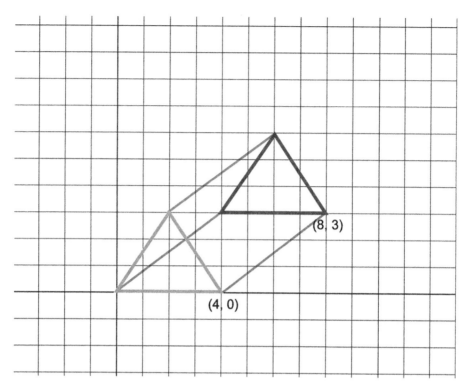

Figure 4-5. *Translating the x and y coordinates of a triangle's vertices moves the triangle without rescaling or reorienting the triangle's original shape*

$$\begin{bmatrix} p_x & p_y & p_z \end{bmatrix} \cdot \begin{bmatrix} 1 & 0 & v_x \\ 0 & 1 & v_y \\ 0 & 0 & v_z \end{bmatrix} = \begin{bmatrix} p_x + v_x \\ p_y + v_y \\ p_z + v_z \end{bmatrix} = \begin{bmatrix} x_2 \\ y_2 \\ z_2 \end{bmatrix}$$

Figure 4-6. *The variables Vx, Vy, and Vz represent the values of a translation in matrix form. Multiplying a vector of coordinates with a translation matrix returns the vector's coordinates following translation*

Matrix multiplication with a vector follows a simple rule. We multiply each element of a row in the vector with each element of the corresponding column in the matrix, and then add the results (Figure 4-7). The outcome is a new vector of x, y, and z coordinates that represents the destination of each original vertex after the move.

$$\begin{bmatrix} x & y & z \end{bmatrix} \cdot \begin{bmatrix} 1 & 2 & 3 \\ 4 & 5 & 6 \\ 7 & 8 & 9 \end{bmatrix} =$$

$$x_2 = x(1) + y(4) + z(7)$$

$$y_2 = x(2) + y(5) + z(8)$$

$$z_2 = x(3) + y(6) + z(9)$$

Figure 4-7. *An illustration showing the mechanics of vector-matrix multiplication*

Scaling

In addition to translating a set of vertices, multiplying a vector of coordinates by a matrix can scale an object in 2D or 3D space.

Whereas a translation operation adds the size of the movement to a vector's original coordinates, a scaling operation multiplies the size of the movement with the vector's original coordinates (Figure 4-8). By simply rearranging the order of data in the matrix, and following the rules of matrix-vector multiplication, we can create a different transformation of our vertices (Figure 4-9).

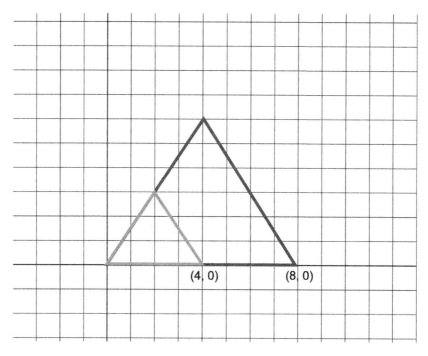

Figure 4-8. *Multiplying a triangle's vertices with a scaling matrix returns a similar triangle either greater or smaller in size*

$$
\begin{bmatrix} p_x & p_y & p_z \end{bmatrix} \cdot \begin{bmatrix} v_x & 0 & 0 \\ 0 & v_y & 0 \\ 0 & 0 & v_z \end{bmatrix} = \begin{bmatrix} p_x . v_x \\ p_y . v_y \\ p_z . v_z \end{bmatrix}
$$

Figure 4-9. *Changing the location of Vx, Vy, and Vz in a matrix multiplied with a vector of coordinates returns a different kind of transformation, in this case a scaling instead of a translation*

Rotation

Rotation, too, is a transformation of vertices that a matrix can package in its rows and columns. Unlike translation and scaling operations, however, rotating shapes in two and three dimensions requires the application of not only arithmetic but also trigonometry.

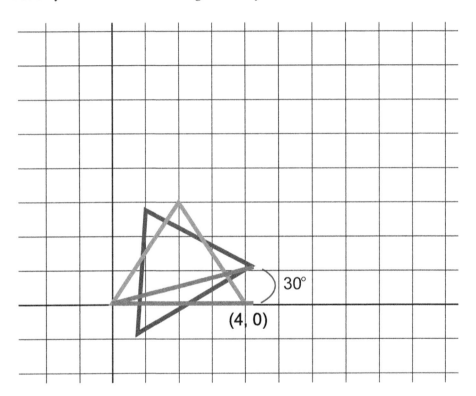

Figure 4-10. *A diagram of a triangle's rotation around the z-axis by 30 degrees*

First, the axis of rotation for a shape is the axis around which it spins. Second, the amount a shape rotates around an axis is its angle of rotation, commonly represented by the Greek character theta, and measured in either radians or degrees (Figure 4-10).

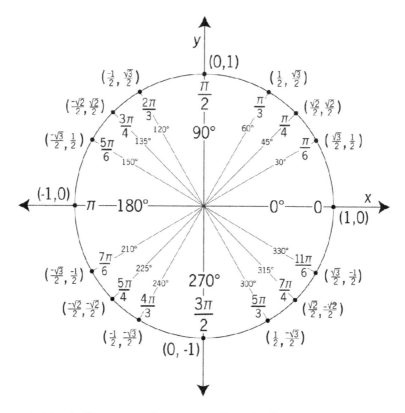

Figure 4-11. *A diagram of a unit circle, which translates a measurement of degrees into radians*

RADIANS AND DEGREES

The circumference of a circle is the measure of its perimeter. The formula $2\pi r$, where r is the radius of the circle, computes the measurement of a circle's circumference. As you likely know, 360 dgrees measures one revolution around a circle. $2\pi r$ is, therefore, the radian expression of 360 degrees, and if we assume the radius is 1, then the expression becomes 2π. Half a circle, 180 degrees, is then π, 90 degrees is $\pi/2$, and 0 degrees is, again, 2π (Figure 4-11).

The relationship between circles and degrees allows us to leverage the fixed nature of circles to compute the rotations of shapes along axes. Intuitively, imagine a line measuring the radius of a circle moving counterclockwise around a circle centered on the origin on an x y plane. Now, imagine dropping a line from the tip of the radius at the circle's edge to the x-axis (Figure 4-12). Let's call this line O. The shape formed by the radius, the line dropped from its tip, O, and the x-axis forms a right triangle wherein the radius defines the hypotenuse. If O remains fixed to the tip of the radius as it moves around the circle, then O will trace the perimeter of the circle, and its length will change in proportion to the length of the triangle's base, side A.

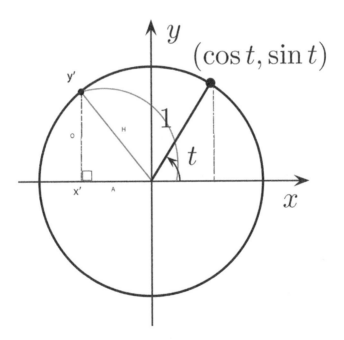

Figure 4-12. *A diagram of right triangles whose hypotenuses are the radius of the circle. The fixed radius means sides O and A of the triangle change in proportion to each other and the angle represented by t, commonly referred to as theta*

Sine, Cosine, Tangent

The dimensions of the triangle are constrained. They are constrained by the fixed length of the radius, or hypotenuse. As the angle between line segments O and A must remain 90 degrees, the only way the triangle can retain its shape is by adjusting the lengths of O and A. Consequently, the lengths of O and A change not only in relation to each other, but also in relation to the angle formed between the hypotenuse and the x-axis. That angle is Θ, pronounced *theta*, the measurement in degrees or radians of the point intersected by the radius and the circle's edge. O is the side of the triangle opposite Θ, and A is the side adjacent to it. If the radius of the circle is also the hypotenuse of a right triangle, then the lengths of sides O and A can be measured using the acronym SOH-CAH-TOA (Figure 4-13).

Where, SOH stands for:

Sin Θ = Opposite over Hypotenuse, or O/H
CAH:
Cosine Θ = Adjacent over Hypotenuse, or A/H
TOA:
Tangent Θ = Opposite/Adjacent, or O/A

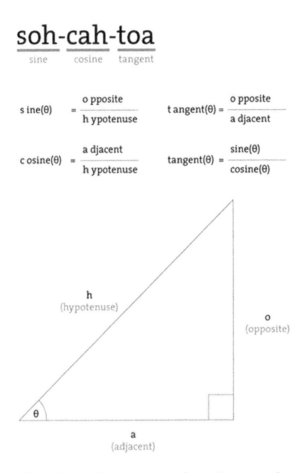

Figure 4-13. *The relative dimensions of a right triangle with angle theta between sides h and a can be calculated with the operations described by the acronym soh-cah-toa*

Sin Θ is a measurement of the y coordinate of a rotation. Cos Θ is a measurement of the x coordinate of a rotation. As one axis will remain fixed during a rotation transformation, cos Θ and sin Θ are the only values our program must compute to calculate the effect of a rotation on a vector of coordinates—theoretically.

Trouble comes quickly when we try to calculate rotations in our 3D scenes with rotation matrices comprising only x, y, and z elements (Figure 4-14). In the example I provided previously, the radius of the circle moved in only two dimensions. Fortunately, a rotation around the z-axis conveniently maps cos Θ and sin Θ values to x and y coordinates after rotation. However, what happens if we try to measure a rotation around the y-axis?

$$
R_x(\theta) = \begin{bmatrix} 1 & 0 & 0 \\ 0 & \cos\theta & -\sin\theta \\ 0 & \sin\theta & \cos\theta \end{bmatrix}
$$

$$
R_y(\theta) = \begin{bmatrix} \cos\theta & 0 & \sin\theta \\ 0 & 1 & 0 \\ -\sin\theta & 0 & \cos\theta \end{bmatrix}
$$

$$
R_z(\theta) = \begin{bmatrix} \cos\theta & -\sin\theta & 0 \\ \sin\theta & \cos\theta & 0 \\ 0 & 0 & 1 \end{bmatrix}
$$

Figure 4-14. *Rotation matrices for each axis, xyz, require calculations of only the sin and cosine of angle theta. Defining rotations in three dimensions with only these matrices, however, leads to unintended problems*

Homogeneous Coordinates and Quaternions

A rotation around the y-axis can be computed in the manner we described using a value called Euler angles. Euler angles are the degree or radian measurements of a line relative to the origin, the point of intersection of the x, y, and z axes. However, problems arise with Euler angles when we try to measure a rotation relative to an axis other than z using the trigonometric functions of Θ. Rotating a cube 90 degrees along the y axis, for example, changes the cube's orientation. What the cube understood to be its x-axis, the axis increasing in value from its right to left after rotation, lines up with the z-axis of the coordinate plane (Figure 4-15). The cosine value of Θ becomes the same for x and z for a 90-degree rotation along the y-axis. An entire degree of freedom has been lost.

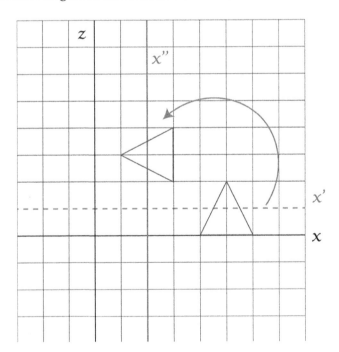

Figure 4-15. *A diagram from a bird's eye view of a triangle rotated around the y-axis. The alignment of the triangle's local x-axis with the global z-axis results in a loss of a degree of freedom called gimbal lock*

The result of axes becoming parallel following a rotation in 3D space is a loss of an axis of movement, otherwise known as gimbal lock. Gimbal lock, together with an assortment of other computational challenges presented by the measurement of 3D rotation in Euler angles, has motivated 3D graphics designers to derive more efficient computation for 3D rotation. One such method involves a fourth dimension of imaginary numbers that take into account a subject's orientation relative to the viewer's frame of reference. The value of the measurement is known as quaternions, and quaternions, by solving the problems introduced by Euler angles, allow 3D developers like us to continue using matrices to represent the values of transformations in our scenes.

From Many into One

The full power of matrix multiplication becomes apparent in the transformation matrix. As the multiplication of a vector of coordinates with a translation, scaling, or rotation matrix executes a transformation of the vector's vertices, the matrix is a document of the transformation. Each matrix is like a map from our analogy that instructed you how to move from my house to a single location. To keep you from having to restart your journey from my house for each leg of your trip, I gave you a map of the town with all routes highlighted. That map was a single document with all of your movement recorded. That map was a transformation matrix. In 3D computer graphics, a transformation matrix codifies all the movement a vertex will perform in one operation. Multiplying a translation, scaling, and rotation matrix together creates a transformation matrix, which when applied to a set of vertices, translates, scales, and rotates the vertices in one operation.

There is a caveat, however. Matrix multiplication is not commutative. The order by which we multiply the matrices matters. Multiplying a vector by a translation matrix and then a rotation matrix creates a different image than multiplying a rotation matrix by a translation matrix. For example, imagine the letter C. Now, flip it across the y-axis, so that it is backward. Then rotate it 90 degrees counterclockwise. The result resembles a bridge. However, rotating the letter C 90 degrees then flipping it across the y axis returns an image more representative of a boat. Order matters to matrix multiplication, and in a scene requiring the motion of millions of vertices, computation quickly becomes inhumanly complex.

Notably, it is not the matrix itself that creates the transformation of a vector of coordinates; it is the information contained within the matrix that describes the transformation to occur. As mathematical constructs, matrices are a convenient tool for expressing operations, especially for 3D graphics, because a) they present data in ways that maintain the fundamental rules of arithmetic, and b) they work very well with the hardware computing architecture of GPUs.

GPUs and Matrices Sitting In a Tree . . .

Recall from an earlier chapter that GPUs differ from CPUs in their number of cores. One feature of GPUs I did not mention is the number of ALUs they contain. Each core of a GPU has its own ALU, an arithmetic-logic unit, which handles arithmetic and logical AND OR operations. Whereas the memory of a chip stores the data and instructions of a program, the ALU performs the computation. The architecture of GPUs gives them the ability to parallelize a task, such as multiplying the rows and columns of matrices simultaneously (Figure 4-16). The unique form and function of both matrices and GPUs allow for blazingly fast calculations, particularly of vertices in 3D space.

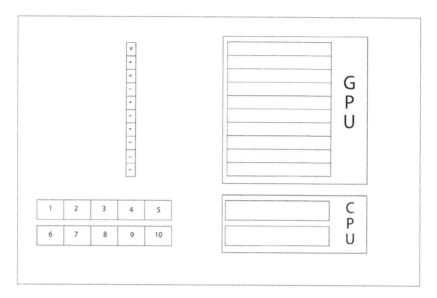

Figure 4-16. *The unique architecture of a GPU allows it to multiply the indices of matrices simultaneously, resulting in the execution of operations at a rate significantly faster than possible in a CPU*

Originally, developers who wished to avail themselves of the power unleashed by parallelized matrix multiplication on GPUs had to write their code in a fashion optimized for multithreaded operations. Fortunately, APIs such as WebGL and CUDA for Nvidia graphics chips, among others, have formalized the automatic compilation of code we write into a format optimized for parallel execution. Matrix multiplication, therefore, is a procedure ideally suited for 3D rendering with GPUs.

Exercise 3, Part 1: Matrix Revolution

In this exercise we will use the arithmetic operation of matrix multiplication in a WebGL program to rotate the three-sided cube we created in Exercise 2. To achieve our aim, we will use a free, open source JavaScript helper library called glMatrix.js, which is comaintained by

Brandon Jones, a Google developer who also serves as an editor of the WebXR specification. By the end of Part 1 of this exercise, you will better understand the power and convenience provided by matrix multiplication in WebGL.

Import GLMatrix.js

1. Open the HTML and JS files from the end of Exercise 2. Alternatively, download the source file for this exercise from the course's GitHub repository, available at `www.apress.com/book/9781484263174`.

2. Navigate to the glMatrix.js source code on the CDNJS website: `https://cdnjs.com/libraries/gl-matrix`.

    CDNJS is a popular, free, and public website that offers developers access to a multitude of JavaScript libraries. Nearly 10% of all websites around the world rely on CDNJS for resources that drive their performance. As a CDN, a content delivery network, CDNJS provides us with a convenient interface to use the code contained in libraries in our programs without downloading or hosting the files on our own machines.

3. On the glMatrix.js page of CDNS, select the drop-down menu to the right of the gl-matrix-min.js file. Select Copy Script Tag (Figure 4-17).

Figure 4-17. *Select Copy Script Tag from the Copy drop-down menu on the gl-Matrix-min.js file on CDNJS*

A minified JS file is one that has been compressed into a format not suitable for humans to read. As we will not concern ourselves with the low-level details of the glMatrix.js library in this exercise, the minified version of the code serves our needs. The version available as of this writing is version 2.8.1.

4. Return to the code editor where you've opened the HTML and JS files for this exercise. Immediately above the closing </html> tag in the index.html document, and just below the <script> tag for the previous lesson's JavaScript source file, paste the script tag you copied from the CDNJS gl-Matrix-min.js page.

```
<script src="ch4_ex2-3.js"></script>
<script src="https://cdnjs.cloudflare.com/ajax/libs/
gl-matrix/2.8.1/gl-matrix-min.js" integrity="sha256-
+O9xst+d1zIS41eAvRDCXOfOMH993E4cS4OhKBIJj8Q="
crossorigin="anonymous"></script>
</html>
```

5. Rename or copy the code from the JS file completed
    at the end of Exercise 2, Part 3 into a file you save
    as lesson3-1.js. After making sure the new JS file
    shares a folder with your index.html page for this
    exercise, redefine the src address for the home
    page's main JavaScript file.

```
Old script tag: <script src="ch4_ex2-3.js"></script>
New script tag: <script src="lesson3-1.js"></script>
```

Uniforms in Shaders

The first change we will make to our renamed JavaScript file is in the code
for the vertex shader source.

1. Add a uniform mat4 property named
    uModelViewMatrix to the string defining the
    vsSource variable.

```
const vsSource = '
    attribute vec4 aPosition;
    attribute vec4 aVertexColor;

    uniform mat4 uModelViewMatrix;
    ...
```

Whereas an attribute qualifier defines input unique to a vertex shader
in WebGL, a uniform qualifier defines an input property shared between
a vertex and fragment shader. The mat4 uniform we have added to our
code informs the GPU to reserve enough contiguous memory to store
a matrix data structure with four rows and four columns. Unlike a vec4
attribute defining a color value, however, the fourth index in both the
row and column of a mat4 data structure used for vertex transformation is
not reserved for an alpha, or opacity, value. While the first three elements

of each row and column hold x, y, and z coordinates, like the aPosition attribute, the fourth element is a value called *w*, which conventionally represents the direction of an object in quaternions. The value of the fourth index in a vec4 attribute like aPosition is also a value for *w*. A mat4 matrix structure, therefore, allows us to calculate the position attribute of a vertex with a matrix to define translation, scaling, and especially rotation using quaternions.

QUATERNIONS VS. EULER ANGLES

Quaternions differ from Euler angles as measurements of an object's rotation in space because of their inclusion of a fourth coordinate, *w*. XYZ vectors in 3D space can refer to either a position, located at the point of the vector, or a direction. For example, in physics a vector measurement of force has both a quantity *and* a direction. Gravity is a force that has a quantity (9.8 m/s²) *and* a direction, down. In a quaternion, *w* describes whether a vector represents a position, a quantity, or a direction. When *w* = 0, a quaternion represents a direction. When *w* = 1, a quaternion represents a position. The use of the *w* value in 3D graphics allows us to reorient vertices without translating them, a feature that conveniently avoids gimbal lock. For further reference on the derivation of the value referenced by the variable *w*, search for resources on homogenous coordinates.[2]

The Order of Floperations

As we covered in this chapter's introduction multiplying a vector of a vertex's coordinates with a certain kind of matrix transforms the position, scale, and/or orientation of the vertex. One concept we touched on only briefly is

---

[2]One helpful resource may be the YouTube video *Math for Game Developers - Homogeneous Coordinates* by Jorge Rodriguez.

matrix concatenation. The primary reason matrices increase the speed of complex 3D operations is their property of concatenation. To concatenate matrices means to multiply them together to preserve the total movement held within each matrix. Multiplying three matrices—for example, a rotation, scaling, and translation matrix—returns a single matrix that holds the final orientation, size, and position to be applied to a vertex. A matrix that holds the product of other transformations is called a *transform.*

The order in which we multiply matrices during concatenation matters a great deal. Unlike multiplication between scalars, like integers, multiplication between matrices is *not* commutative. That means multiplying the same matrices in different orders will return different results. In this odd circumstance, 2 × 3 may equal 6 but 3 × 2 will not. We define the order of the multiplication in the main() method of the vertex shader's source code.

1. In the string saved into the target variable vsSource, multiply the uniform matrix by the position attribute.

    ```
    void main() {
            gl_Position = uModelViewMatrix * aPosition;
            vColor = aVertexColor;
        }
    ```

    Multiplying the aPosition vector, the XYZ coordinates of a vertex, by the ModelViewMatrix uniform *transforms* the vertex's state by the values within the ModelViewMatrix. Because this operation occurs inside our vertex shader, the shader program will run it once for each vertex. Whatever values we place in the ModelViewMatrix, therefore, will determine the rotation, scale, and position of each vertex in our scene.

As we have only added a uniform qualifier to our vertex shader, we do not need to change any code creating, compiling, or linking our shaders. However, as we did with the position and color attributes of the vertex shader, we must provide the GPU with an address for our uniform values in memory. Further, we have to create and store the data the uniform `mat4` data structure will hold.

2. In the section of the JS file where we connected attributes with the vertex shader, create a variable to store the location of the uniform matrix linked to the shader program.

```
const modelMatrixLocation = gl.getUniformLocation
(program, 'uModelViewMatrix');
```

At this point in our code, the program connected with the WebGL context on our home page has a location in memory of our `mat4` data structure.

Making Memories of Matrices

However, the memory holds no data in the matrix. We create the data by instantiating a 4×4 matrix using code from the `glMatrix` library.

1. Create a target variable to store a 4×4 identity matrix beneath the declaration of the `modelMatrixLocation` variable.

```
const modelViewMatrix = mat4.create();
```

Because the value of the `modelViewMatrix` we created is equivalent to 1, the identity matrix, the `modelViewMatrix` will not impact the rotation, scale, or position of our scene's vertices.

Next, as we did with the attribute values in the vertex shader, we inform the gl context of the location of our mat4 data in memory and connect it with the values we'd like it to store.

2. Call the gl.uniformMatrix4fv() function with the following parameters to fully connect the GPU's program with the four float values we've stored in each column of the matrix uniform.

```
gl.uniformMatrix4fv(modelMatrixLocation,
false, modelViewMatrix);
```

If you save the HTML and JS files we've so far edited in this exercise and load them into a browser through a local server, you may be surprised by the appearance of a blank page. Opening the console window of the browser (CTRL + SHIFT + I in Chrome/Edge) reveals any errors encountered by the browser while loading our program. If you've followed along with the steps in this exercise, you may see in your console the following Reference Error: mat4 is undefined. This is an odd error for us to receive, because we've clearly linked to the glMatrix library, which defines the mat4 object, in our index.html.

```
<script src="lesson3-1.js"></script>
<script src="https://cdnjs.cloudflare.com/ajax/libs/gl-matrix/
2.8.1/gl-matrix-min.js" integrity="sha256-+09xst+d1zIS41eAvRDCX
0f0MH993E4cS40hKBIJj8Q=" crossorigin="anonymous"></script>
```

But here is a valuable lesson to learn about the browser's parsing of an HTML document.

Order in the Import

As we've referenced the JS file containing the WebGL program above the glMatrix CDNS source in our HTML, the browser's JS engine encounters an error during compilation. Because it has yet to compile the code inside the glMatrix library the JS engine has no knowledge of the mat4 object, its properties, or methods, such as create(). The remedy is simple:

1. Swap the order of the script tags in index.html.

    ```
    <script src="https://cdnjs.cloudflare.com/
    ajax/libs/gl-matrix/2.8.1/gl-matrix-min.js"
    integrity="sha256-+O9xst+d1zIS41eAvRDCXOfOMH993E4
    cS4OhKBIJj8Q=" crossorigin="anonymous"></script>
    ```

    ```
    <script src="lesson3-1.js"></script>
    ```

Saving index.html and reloading it in the browser should show a familiar image: a tricolored, three-faced cube.

But isn't this the exact same image from the end of the previous chapter's exercise? Yes, it is! So what have we accomplished? Nothing! Huh?

Who Am I?

Though we've added a uniform qualifier to our shader source, created a 4×4 matrix, provided it values, and saved it in memory, we have not actually *done* anything to the vertices in our scene. Yes, we multiplied the uniform matrix by the attribute aPosition in our vertex shader, but what did that really accomplish? The answer is nothing.

The function we called on the mat4 object to create the 4×4 matrix that we saved as a uniform in our shader pipeline by default creates an operand called an identity matrix. An identity matrix is one that acts as the number 1 in multiplication; multiplying a 4×4 matrix **A** by a 4×4 identity matrix, for example **I**, returns matrix **A**. In the main() function of our vertex shader we defined the gl_Position property as the product of a vector of coordinates and an identity matrix. As is the case with multiplication between any positive integer and the number 1, the result is our original vector of coordinates. In short, nothing in our scene has transformed.

Making Moves with Matrices

To effect movement in our scene, let's first add code to our WebGL program to translate the polygon up the y-axis.

1. In the JS file for the exercise, beneath the line where we declared the `modelViewMatrix` variable and instantiated it with a 4×4 identity matrix, add the following `glMatrix` method:

    ```
    mat4.translate();
    ```

    According to the `glMatrix` documentation, the `mat4.translate()` function takes three parameters: 1) the destination matrix, 2) the matrix to translate, and 3) the amount to translate as a vector. For this step in the exercise, we will translate the polygon in our scene up the y-axis 0.5 coordinates.

2. Add the following parameters between the parentheses of the `mat4.translate()` function:

    ```
    mat4.translate(modelViewMatrix,  // destination matrix
             modelViewMatrix,       // matrix to translate
             [0.0, 0.5, 0.0]);      // amount to translate
    ```

After saving and reloading the scene, you should see our tricolored polygon translated to a position above its previous one.

But at the start of this exercise I promised you a cube that rotates, and translating a cube, while cool, doesn't fulfill that promise. However, before we can begin spinning our cube in our scene, we must answer a fundamental question posed by any kind of animation: how do we capture the passage of time?

Animation

Most ten-year olds probably know animation is a series of still images projected quickly in sequence. As we covered in the earlier chapters of this book, our Web browsers also project a series of still images quickly in sequence. The rate of projection of a Web browser, as well as of the screens through which we view them, is a measurement of frames per a second, or fps. Fortunately, as Web developers, we don't have to concern ourselves with the details of how a browser refreshes itself; the act is autonomic, like breathing for humans.

I Think There for Loop

Yet, though the browser computes its own refresh rate it also provides developers with the option to peek into its process. By hooking our WebGL program into the browser's automatic refresh rate, we can instruct the browser's rendering engine to redraw our scene differently for every frame. In the final steps of Part 1 of this exercise, we will create a recursive loop: a function that calls itself, to continuously update the state of our scene's vertices for every frame the browser draws.

To begin, we'll need to ask ourselves what stage of our program we would like to execute repeatedly.

```
function main() {
        /*===== Create a WebGL Context ==============*/

        /*===== Define and Store the Geometry ======*/

        /*===== Shaders ============================*/

        /*===== Supply the data to the GPU =========*/

        /*===== Drawing ============================*/
}
```

Recall that the WebGL pipeline is a state machine. As such, it does not require reassembly every frame. The pipeline takes as input the parameters of our shaders, executes the shader programs on the GPU, and draws the points and colors to the screen. Because we are using matrix multiplication to move the vertices of our scene, we can rely on the shaders to calculate the correct state of our polygon for each frame. However, as the coordinates of our vertices *will* change, and by extension the color of their pixels on our screens, we must refresh the buffers holding our uniform and attributes. Since we perform these operations in the phase of our WebGL program prior to drawing, we will begin the recursive loop there.

1. Below the line on which you call `gl.useProgram(program)`, inside the curly braces of the `main()` function, define a function called render and pass in a parameter named now.

   ```
   function render(now) {

   }
   ```

2. Between the curly braces of the render function, copy and paste the code from `gl.useProgram()` to the closing brace of the `main()` function, including the `gl.drawArrays()` method.

   ```
   ...
   gl.useProgram(program);

   /*=========== Connect the attributes with the vertex
   shader ===========*/
   const posAttribLocation = gl.getAttribLocation(program,
   "aPosition");
   gl.bindBuffer(gl.ARRAY_BUFFER, origBuffer);
   gl.vertexAttribPointer(posAttribLocation, 3, gl.FLOAT,
   false, 0, 0);
   ```

```
gl.enableVertexAttribArray(posAttribLocation);

const colorAttribLocation =
gl.getAttribLocation(program, "aVertexColor");
gl.bindBuffer(gl.ARRAY_BUFFER, colorBuffer);
gl.vertexAttribPointer(colorAttribLocation, 4,
gl.FLOAT, false, 0, 0);
gl.enableVertexAttribArray(colorAttribLocation);

const modelMatrixLocation =
gl.getUniformLocation(program, 'uModelViewMatrix');

const modelViewMatrix = mat4.create();

mat4.translate(modelViewMatrix,    // destination matrix
               modelViewMatrix,    // matrix to translate
               [0.0, 0.5, 0.0]);   // amount to translate

gl.uniformMatrix4fv(modelMatrixLocation, false,
modelViewMatrix);

/*========== Drawing ========== */
gl.clearColor(1, 1, 1, 1);

gl.enable(gl.DEPTH_TEST);
//gl.depthFunc(gl.LEQUAL);

gl.clear(gl.COLOR_BUFFER_BIT | gl.DEPTH_BUFFER_BIT);

// Draw the points on the screen
const mode = gl.TRIANGLES;
const first = 0;
const count = 18;
gl.drawArrays(mode, first, count);
}
```

As our goal in this exercise is to animate a polygon that rotates, we can't simply multiply our vertices with an identity matrix and expect results. **Instead, we must write functions that inform the renderer of how much the vertices in our scene move in each frame**.

Reaching Rotation with Real Radical Radians

From the analogy that opened this chapter, we know that a rotation matrix holds the information for how much vertices should rotate; we also know that multiplying a vector with a rotation matrix will rotate the points of the vector.

1. Delete the mat4.translate() function you created in a previous step and replace it with a rotation function also defined in the glMatrix library.

```
mat4.rotate(modelViewMatrix,   // destination matrix
      modelViewMatrix,         // matrix to rotate
      cubeRotation,            // amount to rotate in
                                  radians
      [0, 0, 1]);             // axis to rotate around (Z)
```

Unlike the translate function, which accepts three parameters, the mat4.rotate() function accepts four parameters. While the first two remain identical, the last two are unique to calling rotation on a matrix. The final parameter, the axis of rotation, is self-explanatory, where the number 1 marks the desired axis as true. The third parameter, however, hearkens back to our discussion of trigonometry.

Recall that radians define the degrees of rotation around the unit circle as real numbers in terms of Pi. As real numbers, radians compute conveniently as decimals in the GPU. The variable `cubeRotation` defines the rate of rotation for our vertices: how many radians, or degrees, we'd like our cube to rotate between frames. However, to reference the variable in our `render(now)` function, we must first define it.

2. Just above the declaration of the render(now) function, create the variable `cubeRotation` and set its value to 0.0.

```
let cubeRotation = 0.0;
```

Because we require our render(now) function to be recursive, we call it again at the bottom of its own declaration.

3. Below the `gl.drawArrays()` method call, yet above the closing bracket of the render function declaration, call the function `requestAnimationFrame()` with the name of the render function passed in as a parameter.

```
requestAnimationFrame(render);
```

A browser provides access to the `requestAnimationFrame()` function through its Window interface. Each tab in a browser has its own window object, which in turn holds a document object, the tree data structure the browser's engines use to parse and render the page. The function `window.requestAnimationFrame()` informs the browser that our program would like to perform an action on the data supplying our page to update its state, or appearance, before the window's next repainting.

Callback, Maybe

The parameter `requestAnimationFrame()` accepts is known as a callback, a function scheduled to be called by the program immediately upon the execution of another task. In our example, by passing render as its callback parameter, `requestAnimationFrame()` notifies the browser to rerender our page upon the next refresh, which occurs about 60 times a second, depending on the display refresh rate of the browser. Implicit in the callback accepted by `window.requestAnimationFrame()` is a timestamp in milliseconds of when in the window's lifecycle the `requestAnimationFrame()` function was called. We've already defined this parameter with the variable "now" in our render function declaration. Save the `lesson3-1.js` file and reload the home page in your browser. What do you see?

Hopefully you see nothing: a blank, white page inside your browser window. Asking "why" completes our understanding of the animation loop.

Animation Loop

The execution of our JavaScript program occurs like this: the browser parses our HTML document; noticing a JavaScript file before the closing `</html>` tag, the browser sets its JS engine to compiling our JS code; following compilation, the browser's JS engine runs the code, beginning with the first function call, which in our program is `main()`; the program completes, however, without rendering anything to the page. The reason our render function does not execute inside the browser is because, though we define it, we never call it *inside* the main function. I belabor the point because it provides a clear, simple example of the often confusing concept in JS called scope.

Scope in JavaScript

An analogy for scope is an image of wooden, nested dolls, one inside another decreasing in size. One way to conveniently recognize the beginning and end of a scope in a JS program is to follow the opening and closing of curly braces. An opening brace creates a new scope and its corresponding closing brace ends it. Scopes define the life cycles of variables in programs. A variable created between two curly braces cannot exist outside them. The deletion of a variable once its scope has closed is called garbage collection. Garbage collection is a process used by some programming languages like JavaScript to efficiently manage the memory requested and freed by a program. A variable can be accessed by scopes at or beneath its level. However, variables defined within nested scopes, or smaller dolls, cannot be accessed by higher scopes, or larger dolls, that contain them.

In the last step of this exercise, we called `requestAnimationFrame` (`render`) from *inside* the render function declaration, a scope our program does not reach. To gain access to the code within the scope of the render function, between its curly braces, we must call the function from a scope available to `main()`.

1. Call `requestAnimationFrame(render)` outside the closing curly brace of the render function declaration, just above the closing brace of the main function declaration.

    ```
        ....
        requestAnimationFrame(render);
      }
      requestAnimationFrame(render);
    } // ← closing brace for function main()
    ```

Saving `lesson3-1.js` and reloading the home page in the browser should show an image of our cube. Why hasn't anything changed?

DeltaTime

In order for animation to occur in a browser, the renderer must repaint the canvas context each frame with updated components. Though we've called the function to repaint the context in our program, in the proper scope, we have not provided the program with a way to distinguish "this" point in time from "that" point in time. Conventionally, a change in time is marked as the delta between moments. By saving the value of the time delta in a variable for each frame update of the program, we can "move" the vertices in our scene using arithmetic—from "then" to "now."

1. Just above the render function definition, declare a variable.

    ```
    let then = 0;
    ```

2. Inside the render function, at the top of its scope, declare a variable to hold the change in time between animation frames; set the state of now and then.

    ```
    now *= 0.001;  // convert milliseconds to seconds
    let deltaTime = now - then;
    then = now;
    ```

3. Finally, between gl.drawArrays() and requestAnimationFrame() inside the render function's scope, calculate the vertices' rate of rotation per frame using the "+=" operator, which translates to "equals itself plus."

    ```
    ...
    gl.drawArrays(mode, first, count);
    cubeRotation += deltaTime;
    requestAnimationFrame(render);
    } // ← closing brace of render function
    ```

Save and run the program in the browser. If the image you see matches that of Figure 4-18, then you have animated vertices in WebGL. Success!

Figure 4-18. *Calling the* render() *function recursively through* requestAnimationFrame() *changes the cube's rotation value every frame*

Part 1 Recap

In Part 1 of this exercise you learned how to include a reference to a third-party JS library through CDN; construct a matrix rotation using the glMatrix helper library; and animate the WebGLRenderingContext by recursively calling requestAnimationFrame() with a callback to render(now). You now understand the basics of 3D animation in WebGL.

However, the rotating polygon in our scene still appears to lack depth. Though it's rotating, it does so along the z-axis, to which we, the viewer, are perpendicular. Watching a cube rotate head-on doesn't provide us with the illusion of depth. Yet, in the real world even staring at an object head-on betrays depth. So, what's going on?

In Part 2 of this exercise we will add a second axis of rotation to the polygon in our scene. We will also use matrix multiplication to create a "camera" with perspective. The additions to our program, a second dimension of rotation and a perspective camera matrix, will make clearer how movement and perspective collaborate in the virtual world to model the optical properties of the real.

Orthographic and Perspective Matrix Projections

We began our study of WebGL with the assumption that the vertex shader renders points to a screen between coordinate values of -1 and 1 on the x, y, and z axes. The outer vertices define the corners of the *canonical view volume*, which correspond to values defined as normalized device coordinates (NDCs).[3] The effect of the vertex shader's transformation of vertices in the "world" of our scene to NDCs in a canonical view volume standardizes the appearance of a scene on screens of different dimensions. The result is a projection of the model view, a vertex's XYZ coordinates, into a world view.

However, as the GPU hardware of a machine renders three dimensions onto a screen's two dimensions, a vertex's z-coordinate value in model, or local, space is lost.[4] The image seen by a user of a scene projected through a view matrix that removes the relative relation of vertices' z-coordinates is one that appears to lack depth. But in our previous example we took pains to paint a square with a higher z-coordinate value in front of one with a lower value. The order of our rasterization was correct. Why then does our image still appear to lack depth?

The answer lies in the distinction between two kinds of 3D projections. One projection is orthographic, while the other is perspective. The creation of the canonical view volume by the operation of the vertex shader in the WebGL pipeline is a projection of the first kind, orthographic. An orthographic projection is one in which the z-coordinates of the scene merge on to the same plane. Though our example in Part 1 of this exercise avails itself of vertices' z-coordinates, its rendering function paints one square atop another on the same 2D surface. Our scene, therefore, quite literally has no depth.

---

[3]Tomas Akenine-Moller and Eric Haines, *Real-Time Rendering,* 2nd Edition (A.K. Peters, 2002), p. 60.

[4]Akenine-Moller & Haines, *Real-Time Rendering,* 58.

A fundamental feature of an orthographic projection is the retention of parallel lines through the transformation. In other words, parallel lines, in a scene following multiplication of its vertices with an orthographic matrix, remain parallel; there is no illusion of perspective. You may recall from art classes you've taken in the past that perspective is the technique developed by Renaissance artists to create the illusion of depth in painting. The key component to the success of perspective rendering is the appearance of parallel lines moving toward inevitable union at the vanishing point. As XR developers, we can recreate the power of perspective in our 3D scenes through the multiplication of a model's vertices with a projection matrix.

The View Frustum

The distinctions between an orthographic and projection matrix are the projection matrix's retention of a vertex's z-value *and* the application of the homogeneous coordinate, *w*. Viewing a scene through a perspective camera, one which applies the projection matrix to a scene's model view coordinates, mimics the physical features of a pinhole camera. By calculating the relationship between a camera's aspect ratio, near-clipping plane, far-clipping plane, and focal length, a perspective matrix in WebGL transforms a 3D scene from an orthographic to a perspective projection as if viewed through a frustum (Figure 4-19). The end result is a scene in which parallel lines appear to vanish toward a point at the horizon line, an effect that renders vertices and pixels on a screen more in line with our human vision of the world.

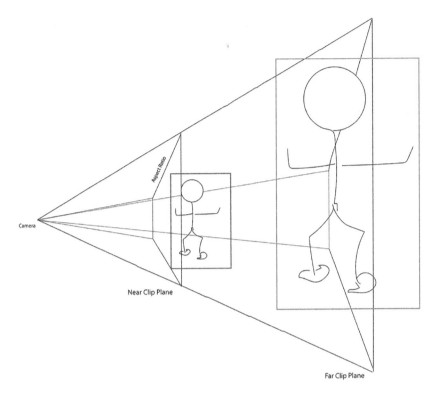

Figure 4-19. *A view frustum, akin to a pyramid with its peak chopped off, transforms vertices between its clipping planes into a bounding box that creates the illusion of perspective*

In Part 2 of this chapter's exercise, we will use the glMatrix.js library to project our rotating cube through a perspective matrix. Then, we will add a second axis of rotation to make it most clear that we've achieved our goal of creating an animated, 3D scene entirely from JavaScript and WebGL.

Exercise 3, Part 2: A Change in Perspective

We ended Part 1 of this exercise with a WebGL JavaScript program that rendered a three-faced, tricolored polygon to the WebGLRenderingContext with an orthographic projection. In the following steps we will replace our scene's orthographic view with one that provides perspective.

Update the Shader Source

1. Copy the JS file from Part 1 of this exercise and rename it `lesson3-2.js`.

2. In the index.html file you've used as the home page for the exercise, replace the JS file linked in the script tag with the relative file path for the JS file `lesson3-2.js`.

3. Add a projection matrix uniform to the vertex shader source code in `lesson3-2.js`.

```
const vsSource = `
    attribute vec4 aPosition;
    attribute vec4 aVertexColor;

    uniform mat4 uModelViewMatrix;
    uniform mat4 uProjectionMatrix;

    varying lowp vec4 vColor;

    void main() {
        gl_Position = uProjectionMatrix *
        uModelViewMatrix * aPosition;
        vColor = aVertexColor;
    }
`;
```

4. Also in the vertex shader source code, multiply the `uModelViewMatrix` uniform and the `aPosition` attribute with the `uProjectionMatrix` uniform. Save the result in the `gl_Position` target variable and be mindful of the order in which you multiply the transforms, as multiplication is not commutative between matrices.

Gaining Perspective

1. Immediately preceding the line of code that
   creates the modelViewMatrix in the "*Connect the*
   attribute with the vertex shader" section of
   the JS code, use the glMatrix.js library to construct
   a 4×4 perspective matrix.

```
// note: glmatrix.js always has the first argument
// as the destination to receive the result.
mat4.perspective(projectionMatrix,
                  fieldOfView,
                  aspect,
                  zNear,
                  zFar);
```

2. As we've provided five variables as arguments to
   the mat4.perspective() function, let's create and
   define the variables in a block of code above the
   function.

```
const fieldOfView = 45 * Math.PI / 180;    // in radians
const aspect = gl.canvas.clientWidth / gl.canvas.
clientHeight;
const zNear = 0.1;
const zFar = 100.0;
const projectionMatrix = mat4.create();
```

For the purposes of this elementary exercise, we may imagine the
values of the variables we created to be defaults. The fieldOfView variable
stores the value of the perspective camera's angle of vision; aspect
stores the aspect ratio of the scene, defined here as the dividend of the
WebGLRenderingContext's width over its height, which maps to the

dimensions of the camera's near clipping plane; zNear holds the distance of the frustum's near-clipping plane from the camera lens, or the viewer's eye; zFar stores the value of the frustum's far-clipping plane, which for all intents and purposes we've set to a value representing infinity; and the variable projectionMatrix holds the 4x4 matrix created by the glMatrix function mat4.create().

Storing the Matrix

Saving and reloading the browser will not apply the perspective matrix to our scene, even though we've defined it and multiplied it in the vertex shader. Recall from Part 1 of this exercise that uniforms, like attributes, defined in code must be connected to the location where their data is stored on the hardware.

1. Create a reference to store the location of the projectionMatrix's uniform data by calling the WebGL function gl.getUniformLocation(), as we did in Part 1 for the modelViewMatrix.

    ```
    const projMatrixLocation =
    gl.getUniformLocation(program,
    'uProjectionMatrix');
    const modelMatrixLocation =
    gl.getUniformLocation(program,
    'uModelViewMatrix'); // defined in Part 1
    ```

2. Immediately above the same code we wrote for the modelViewMatrix in Part 1, connect the uniform data with the empty 4x4 projectionMatrix we created in step 6.

    ```
    gl.uniformMatrix4fv(projMatrixLocation,
    false, projectionMatrix);
    ```

3. Add a second rotation matrix defining rotation around the x-axis to better demonstrate the effect of the perspective matrix on the scene.

```
mat4.rotate(modelViewMatrix,  // destination matrix
      modelViewMatrix,  // matrix to rotate
      cubeRotation,// amount to rotate in radians
      [0, 1, 0]);      // axis to rotate around (X)
```

Saving and reloading the page in the browser will likely reveal an uncomfortably close point of view of the rotating cube. As the perspective matrix projection orients the perspective camera in our scene at the origin, the 0.3 values we provided as the z-coordinate location for some of our vertices pushes the cube out of the frustum of our scene.

Culling and the Model Transform

The WebGL rendering pipeline removes vertices outside the viewing box defined by the frustum through a process called *culling*. To reset the vertices inside the frustum, we can use a translation matrix to move the model transform of our cube further back into our scene.

1. Above the code that defines the rotation matrices around the x and z axes, create and define a translation matrix that moves the cube's vertices back along the z-axis. The rendering pipeline will rasterize the vertices to appear further in front of the camera in our scene.

```
mat4.translate(modelViewMatrix,   // destination matrix
            modelViewMatrix,   // matrix to translate
            [0.0, 0.0, -2.0]); // amount to translate
```

Saving and reloading the scene should render our three-sided, tricolored cube fully in frame of the perspective camera; its rotation along both the z and x axes should make clear that the perspective matrix bends the cube's parallel lines toward a vanishing point at the horizon line (Figure 4-20).

Figure 4-20. *A polygon rendered through orthographic projection (left). The same polygon rendered through perspective projection (right)*

Part 2 Recap

Part 1 of this chapter concluded with a 3D object rendered in our browser that we could not tell was 3D. To help make the depth of the scene clearer, we added three features to our script in Part 2. One feature we added was a second axis of rotation for the cube. The second feature we added was a perspective matrix to replace the orthographic projection through which we viewed our scene. The third feature we added to the program may have been less obvious. It was a transform, a matrix (in our case a vector, a 1×1 matrix) holding a map for movement to apply to the vertices in our scene, stored in the modelViewMatrix. Translating the modelViewMatrix in the last section of the exercise, we moved our "model" two units away from our point of view along the z-axis. Note that we moved the coordinates *inside* our scene: those making up the cube, and *not* the camera matrix. Therefore, we moved the model of our cube *relative* to the viewpoint of the perspective camera. Beginning to understand this concept of relative motion between world and local coordinate spaces now will help your understanding of relative reference spaces in later chapters on immersive interaction.

Summary

At the start of this chapter, linear algebra may have seemed outside the realm of your understanding. Hopefully, by now, you better understand the role linear algebra, specifically matrix multiplication, plays in the rendering of 3D scenes in computer hardware. The WebGL API is as convenient and powerful as it is because of its embrace of both matrix math and the low-level implementation of the graphics rendering pipeline by the drivers of a GPU. It simplifies a great deal of the OpenGL ES specification, and its bindings with JavaScript make it a perfect partner in the Web.

However, as we've found in this chapter particularly, programming through the WebGL API requires a great deal of syntax. The amount of code we generated in this chapter's exercise only rendered half a cube. You can easily imagine the number of lines our JS file would reach if we were to input every vertex of every polygon we'd like to render in a scene by hand. It's for this reason that libraries and applications have emerged to strip away the mundanity of coding in WebGL. In the following chapters we will leave WebGL behind. The fundamentals it has taught us about the generation of 3D images through the graphics rendering pipeline will serve us well as we move toward creating more complex XR applications with tools that carry more of the heavy load.

Key takeaways include:

- We reviewed the fundamentals of matrix vector multiplication.

- We learned that matrices convey information about movement to vertices.

- The types of movement conveyed by matrices are translation, scaling, and rotation.

- Matrix multiplication allows for the efficient calculation of each type of movement through a single transformation matrix.

- GPU architecture is uniquely suited for matrix multiplication through parallel processes.

- Helper libraries abstract the difficulty of encoding matrix multiplication.

- We can loop a transformation in a WebGL scene by calling the request animation frame method.

- Matrix multiplication transforms a view from orthographic to perspective by recreating the optics of a view frustum.

CHAPTER 5

Diving into Three.js

Until now, we've focused heavily on the intricacies of rendering polygons with WebGL. In this chapter, we leave WebGL and its complex syntax of buffers and attributes and uniforms behind. In its place we will use an open source 3D graphics library written in JavaScript called Three.js.

The exercise in this chapter is broken up into three parts. Part 1 addresses just some of the ways Three.js sits atop WebGL to make more convenient many of the basic operations essential to creating the bedrock of a 3D scene. Part 2 introduces the tools Three.js provides to easily create more detailed 3D scenes, scenes with color, materials, and images. Part 3 illustrates that though Three.js simplifies the use of WebGL, it does not jettison WebGL's technical capabilities. By completing an animated, 3D scene through Parts 1, 2, and 3 in this exercise, you will better understand the creative power WebGL places in your hands, and you will see that it is made all the more useful by the convenience of Three.js

In this chapter you will:

- Learn the relationship between Three.js and WebGL

- Review the graphics rendering pipeline through the lens of Three.js

- Create geometry in Three.js

- Begin an understanding of light objects in Three.js

- Begin an understanding of materials in the lighting model for a scene

© Rakesh Baruah 2021
R. Baruah, *AR and VR Using the WebXR API*,
https://doi.org/10.1007/978-1-4842-6318-1_5

- Learn how to use images as textures on materials to create different effects
- Explore the use of parametric equations to create animation in a Three.js scene

What Is Three.js?

Three.js, as in JavaScript for three-dimensional rendering on the Web, is an open source JavaScript library originally developed by Ricardo Cabello in 2010 and maintained by many others since. Though more than 10 years old, Three.js has come of age during the present era of WebXR. As a library of ready-made classes and functions, Three.js sits atop the WebGL API provided by Web browsers. Three.js doesn't replace WebGL; it doesn't even extend it. So how do Three.js and WebGL coexist? Let's begin with an analogy.

A Synthesizer for Shapes

One way I imagine Three.js to operate in concert with WebGL is as an electronic synthesizer, or keyboard, like one a musician may use to create different kinds of sounds. Three.js is to WebGL as a synthesizer is to an orchestra. Both a synthesizer and an orchestra can create incredible, moving music. One is only better than the other depending on context. It's not the quality of the product that distinguishes a synthesizer from an orchestra, or Three.js from WebGL. The difference lies in complexity. To play each instrument in an orchestra you'd have to know the fingering, notation, and registers for each seat, at least. A synthesizer ports every instrument into one interface familiar to musicians from different backgrounds: the black and white keys of a piano. Three.js is like a synthesizer for WebGL. The functionality and possibilities remain; all that has gone are the strings, different tunings, octave shifts, reeds, brass, and timpani. The music is what's left.

WebGL but Simpler

Fortunately, since Three.js sits atop the WebGL API in the browser, the fundamentals of the graphics rendering pipeline for the Web we covered in the previous chapters remain relevant. As a higher level abstraction of the WebGL API, Three.js simplifies things for the general developer more interested in convenience than fine-tuning. To better understand the similarities and differences between WebGL and Three.js, we will recreate the premise we explored with WebGL: a 3D spinning cube. We'll do this in three parts.

Exercise 4, Part 1: Remix the Matrix

We concluded the previous exercise with a simple Web page that animated a three-face, tricolored cube transformed through a perspective matrix rotating around the z and x axes. Composing the scene using the WebGL API and the glMatrix.js helper library required about 150 lines of code in the editor. Using Three.js, we will recreate a similar scene using 80% fewer lines of JavaScript. In Part 1 of this exercise you will:

- Include Three.js in a VS code project as a Module
- Create a perspective camera object
- Create a scene object
- Create primitive shapes from a geometry constructor
- Apply materials to a shape using a mesh constructor
- Animate an object using an animation loop
- Add a directional light object to a scene
- Correct pixilation of a scene by dynamically updating the framebuffer for the canvas

Download the Three.js Source Code

To download the source code for Three.js, you can copy and paste the raw code from the Three.js GitHub repository, available at the following URL, into a new JS file in your project folder: `https://github.com/mrdoob/Three.js/blob/dev/build/three.module.js?raw=true`.

Another way you can download the Three.js source code to your local machine is as a ZIP file by visiting the URL: `https://github.com/mrdoob/Three.js/archive/master.zip`.

Finally, you can also link to the library using a CDN,[1] as we did to access the gl-matrix.js library; clone the Three.js GitHub repository as explained on the project's GitHub Readme page;[2] or download Three.js as a module using the Node package manager, a process we will discuss more deeply in Chapter 7.

A Detour into ES Modules

In Part 1 of Exercise 3, we accessed a helper library called gl-matrix.js by importing it into our HTML document through a CDN. The advantage was that we didn't have to download and host the file on our own machines for development. The gain was convenience. The cost, however, was limited access to an opaque library. Another option available to developers to host JavaScript libraries inside their applications is the JavaScript module system.

In JavaScript, a module is a script that operates as both a means of storage and delivery (Figure 5-1). It's a CD, a compact disc, in a way; a menu; a box of chocolates. Self-contained, a JS module provides applications access to a select catalog of objects and functions. The contents arrive as bite-size chunks. The result is a main application file into which different JS modules slide like books onto a bookshelf, CDs into a 5-disc changer, or tapes into a tape deck.

---

[1]`https://cdnjs.cloudflare.com/ajax/libs/three.js/r118/three.module.min.js`
[2]`https://github.com/mrdoob/three.js/`

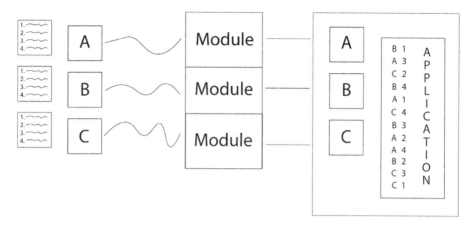

Figure 5-1. *In JavaScript, modules are individual programs whose components can be mixed and matched when imported into an application*

Importing a Module

One popular way of using JS modules is with Node.JS and its package manager, NPM. While it's possible to conveniently import Three.js into our exercise using the Node package manager, we will hold off on introducing the practice until Chapter 7. In this exercise we will focus only on the import of a single JS module, Three.js.

```
<script type="module" src="./index.js"></script>
```

We place the <script> tag near the bottom of our HTML document. We insert the import statement at the top of our main JS script, index. js. By pointing the import command's source to the module folder in our project, we connect all the functionality exported by Three-module.js to our primary JS script. The convenience and efficiency of JS modules will become more apparent as we begin to import more tools to abet our application's functionality.

Importing the Three.js library into our JS script with asterisks (*) tells the server hosting our application that we'd like access to every class and function in the Three.js module. The module pattern for importing scripts allows us to assign all the functionality of the Three.js library to the single variable THREE.

```
import * as THREE from './modules/three.module.js';
```

After downloading and connecting Three.js to our main application, open index.js in your code editor. Here is an outline of the project we will create:

```
main();

function main() {
    // create the context

    // create and set the camera

    // create the scene

    // add fog later...

    // GEOMETRY
        // Create the upright plane

        // Create the cube

        // Create the Sphere

    // MATERIALS and TEXTURES

    // LIGHTS

    // MESH

    // DRAW

    // SET ANIMATION LOOP

    // UPDATE RESIZE
}
```

Making a Context

We begin as we did with our WebGL application, by creating a
`WebGLRendering` context.

Like we did in the previous exercise, connect a `WebGLRendering`
context to the canvas in our HTML document.

```
function main() {
    // create the context
    const canvas = document.querySelector("#c");
    const gl = new THREE.WebGLRenderer({
        canvas,
        antialias: true
    })
    ...
```

Next, we create the camera object in our Three.js scene.

Making a Camera

Three.js offers an assortment of cameras inside its library, but we will
primarily concern ourselves with the perspective camera. The perspective
camera contains the matrix multiplication algorithm that we previously
encoded by hand to project a WebGL scene into perspective.

By first saving the values of the inputs of the target variable, we can
conveniently enter them by variable name.

```
    // create and set the camera
    const angleOfView = 55;
    const aspectRatio = canvas.clientWidth / canvas.clientHeight;
    const nearPlane = 0.1;
    const farPlane = 100;
    const camera = new THREE.PerspectiveCamera(
```

```
    angleOfView,
    aspectRatio,
    nearPlane,
    farPlane
);
camera.position.set(0, 8, 30);
```

The perspective camera object in Three.js has a constructor that accepts a set of inputs called arguments:

- A perspective camera's angle of view is its field of view in radians.

- The aspect ratio is the relationship between the width and height of the viewing window.

- The near plane is the lower boundary of what the rasterizer will allow to appear on screen.

- The far plane value is the upper limit of what the rasterizer will allow to appear in the screen.

Any object not within the lower and upper limits of the camera's planes will be edited by the rasterizer in a process called culling. Finally, calling the set function on the camera's position property allows us to initialize the camera in our scene to a starting position of 8 clicks up the y-axis, and 30 clicks toward us, the viewer.

THE RIGHT HAND RULE

Different 3D systems use one of two coordinate systems. They are identified by the convenient heuristics of the Left Hand and Right Hand Rules. Three.js follows the Right-Hand Rule in establishing its coordinate plane. By forming an "L" with your right thumb and index finger and extending your middle finger, you can visualize the right hand coordinate layout. Point your thumb along the positive direction of the x-axis, parallel to the floor. As Three.js' x-axis rises in value to our right, if we are facing our monitors, its z-axis, represented by your middle finger, moves positively out of the screen, toward us. Your index finger pointing upward is the positive direction of the y-axis from the origin.

Making a Scene

In Three.js, a scene is a data structure that holds its contents as elements or children, just like an HTML document.

With the `WebGLRendering` context and camera values defined, we instantiate the scene of our application with a simple call to the `Scene` object's constructor:

```
// create the scene
const scene = new THREE.Scene();
```

Objects, lights, materials, and textures we add to a scene are stored like ornaments on a Christmas tree.

Geometry

As we learned in Chapter 2, WebGL creates primitive shapes by assembling triangles from the vertex coordinates we provide to the vertex shader through attribute buffers and indices. As a high-level abstraction interface, of sorts, for WebGL, Three.js hides the nuance of geometry creation within constructors of primitive shapes.

Box Geometry

The parameters for the `BoxGeometry` constructor in Three.js are the width, height, and depth of the desired box.

To see how Three.js handles the assembly of vertices into shapes, let's add a cube to our scene.

```
// Create the cube
const cubeSize = 4;
const cubeGeometry = new THREE.BoxGeometry(
    cubeSize,
    cubeSize,
    cubeSize);
```

As a cube is defined by the common value shared by its width, height, and depth, we can create a single variable to hold the cube's dimensions, cubeSize, and pass it into the constructor three times.

Material

An enormous part of the artistry displayed in 3D WebXR scenes derives from the composition of materials. In the context of the graphics rendering pipeline, materials define a parameter in the mathematical equation the shader functions compute on the GPU. Different materials, with different equations, appear differently in scenes beneath lighting. The mathematical relationship between materials and the lights they reflect in a scene comprise what is known as the scene's light model.

The two fundamental materials in Three.js are the Lambert material and the Phong material. The difference between the two materials lies in their unique behavior while interacting with light. A Lambert material reproduces a low-shine, dull quality of light known as diffuse. A Phong material, on the other hand, reproduces a shininess known as the material's specular value.

Phong Material

To better understand the difference between the two materials, let's first apply a Phong material to the cube we've added to our scene.

```
const cubeMaterial = new THREE.MeshPhongMaterial({
    color: 'pink'
});
```

While some constructors accept individual variables, values as arguments, such as the constructor for the perspective camera, other constructors, like that for the Phong material, in Three.js accept what is known as an anonymous JavaScript object.

Anonymous Objects in JavaScript

Identified by curly braces and properties defined through key-value pairs, JavaScript objects provide developers with a tool to create unique objects without the overhead of constructing classes, a practice unavailable in strongly typed languages like C++.

Color is but one property of a Three.js Phong material available for assignment through an anonymous object. For a full catalog of the properties one can define during the construction of a Phong material, refer to the Three.js documentation.

Meshes

You may have noticed in the previous step that the word "mesh" precedes the phrase Phong material in the Three.js constructor. In Three.js, a mesh is an object that unifies the geometry and material of a shape or figure.

Instantiating a mesh for an object in our scene completes the process that began with a call, in this exercise, to the BoxGeometry constructor.

```
const cube = new THREE.Mesh(cubeGeometry, cubeMaterial);
cube.position.set(cubeSize + 1, cubeSize + 1, 0);
scene.add(cube);
```

As we did for the perspective camera in our scene, we can use the set function on the position property of the cube mesh to position the object at a particular location in our scene. Using an arithmetic expression for the x and y coordinates of the cube is a helpful coding technique that provides consistency regardless of the dimensions of the cube.

Rendering Animation

Finally, we define the render function inside the main function of our JS file. Here, we simply add 0.01 to the rotation values around each axis for the cube.

```
// DRAW
function draw(){

    cube.rotation.x += 0.01;
    cube.rotation.y += 0.01;
    cube.rotation.z += 0.01;

    gl.render(scene, camera);
    requestAnimationFrame(draw);
}

    requestAnimationFrame(draw);
} // ← closing brace for main() function
```

As the browser calls requestAnimationFrame() every frame, the draw function we pass as a callback to the function ensures our program runs in a loop that renders the scene about 60 times every second.

Save the JavaScript file and load the application through your local Web server. How does it look?

Painted Black

Unfortunately, your scene at this point, if like mine, appears entirely in black. Why could this be? Let's review what we've done:

1. We created both a canvas and WebGL context on which our application will render our scene.

2. We created a Three.js scene.

3. We created a cube geometry.

4. We created a material for the cube geometry.

5. We wrapped the cube material around the cube geometry, thus creating a mesh for the cube object.

6. We added the cube mesh object to the data structure of our scene.

7. We called the `requestAnimationFrame()` function with a callback to our `draw()` function in which we rotated the cube, and rendered the scene.

The steps are nearly identical to those that we followed while creating a WebGL application in previous exercises. Yet the outcome is unique. It's not that our scene is blank; it has color. The WebGL context is rendering something to the screen—just not our cube. But why?

Let Var Be Light

Recall from earlier in this chapter that the lighting model defines the appearance of a scene in WebGL. Previously, we did not work with materials in WebGL; we worked only with vertices and color values we hard-coded into the fragment shader. In this exercise, by applying a material to a mesh around our cube geometry, we have implicitly asked Three.js to render our scene according to a lighting model—an equation that calculates the appearance of materials in a scene as a function of the light they reflect. We have provided one half of the light model to our scene: the Phong mesh material. Let's add the other half: the light.

Directional Light

Three.js offers four different types of lights for a scene. They are a spotlight, a point light, a hemisphere light, and a directional light. For this exercise, we will use a directional light, which shines in a specific direction through parallel rays.

Beneath the line on which we added the cube mesh to our scene, insert:

```
//LIGHTS
const color = 0xffffff;
const intensity = 1;
const light = new THREE.DirectionalLight(color, intensity);
scene.add(light);
```

The result is even lighting from a source located infinitely far away. Directional lights are commonly used to create the illusion of a sun.

Save and reload the scene, again.

Most likely, you'll see a pink cube rotating in a black void. Our shape had been there all along. The only element missing from the scene was a light to reflect off a material.

Pixel Perfect

Depending on the resolution of your monitor and the dimensions of your browsing window, the cube in your scene may appear heavily pixelated. Though we set the anti-alias property to true in our WebGL context constructor, the scene still suffers from a case of the jaggies.

Dynamically Resizing the Framebuffer

In an earlier exercise we addressed the low resolution of a WebGL scene by hard-coding the size of the framebuffer's dimensions in attributes of the canvas HTML tag. However, in this exercise let's try something more dynamic.

Beneath the closing tag of the main function, create a new function called `resizeGLToDisplaySize(gl)` and pass into it as an argument the variable for our WebGL context, gl. In the body of the function, write the following code:

```
const canvas = gl.domElement;
const width = canvas.clientWidth;
const height = canvas.clientHeight;
const needResize = canvas.width != width || canvas.height
!= height;
if (needResize) {
    gl.setSize(width, height, false);
}
return needResize;
```

Newly introduced in the body of the resize function is the "||" operator. It serves to ask the Boolean question "or". In the syntax of the code we've written, the "||" operator sets the value of the needResize variable to true if either canvas.width or canvas.height properties no longer match their values from the previous frame. Otherwise, the "||" operator sets needResize to false.

The return keyword at the end of the resize function returns the output of the function to the line in the program that called it. Because we want the resize function to evaluate the dimensions of the canvas every frame update, we call it from the beginning of the draw function.

```
// DRAW
function draw(){
    if (resizeGLToDisplaySize(gl)) {
        const canvas = gl.domElement;
        camera.aspect = canvas.clientWidth / canvas.
        clientHeight;
        camera.updateProjectionMatrix();
    } ...
```

Upon saving and reloading the HTML document, you will see that the browser has upgraded its resolution and will upgrade it even when resized.

Upgrading the resolution of the WebGL rendering context for every dimension of the browsing window, creating new geometry, and calculating dynamic lighting on animated materials are but a few of the WebGL functions Three.js streamlines. Yet, what could otherwise appear as magic instead logically extends from the principles of the graphics rendering pipeline we covered throughout the previous chapters. Vertices, perspective, animation, and pixels remain the key ingredients of a WebGL scene, regardless of the instrument creating the painting.

Part 1 Recap

- Created a WebGL rendering context using Three.js as a Module

- Created a scene object that holds the contents of a scene

- Added a perspective camera to a scene

- Added a primitive shape using a geometry constructor built into Three.js

- Applied a Phong material to a shape with a color through a mesh constructor built into Three.js

- Added a directional light to a scene

- Created an animation loop to animate the scene

- Created a function to dynamically update the canvas size to correct pixilation

Exercise 4, Part 2: Materials, Textures

Now that we've recreated the premise of the WebGL exercise that took us four chapters to create in just half of this one, let's continue to leverage the convenience provided by Three.js to flesh-out a full scene. In Part 2 of this chapter's exercise we will augment the scene we have created. In this part of the exercise you will:

- Add plane and sphere geometry to the scene

- Apply two new materials

- Use the Three.js TextureLoader to load image files as texture elements for materials

- Learn how textures and lights can cooperate to create more realistic effects

Sphere Geometry

Let's begin by adding sphere geometry to our scene. Like with the box geometry from Part 1, we create sphere geometry using a Three.js constructor, which accepts as parameters dimensions that define the shape of the sphere we'd like to create.

Inside the main function, in the section marked GEOMETRY, add the following code:

```
// Create the Sphere
const sphereRadius = 3;
const sphereWidthSegments = 32;
const sphereHeightSegments = 16;
const sphereGeometry = new THREE.SphereGeometry(
    sphereRadius,
    sphereWidthSegments,
    sphereHeightSegments
);
```

The width and height segment arguments passed into the SphereGeometry constructor define the number of vertices the vertex shader will use to compute the sphere. The more segments, the smoother the sphere and the more processing power required to render each frame. Play with the values to gain a better understanding of their role, if you'd like.

Lambert Material

As we've only defined the vertices of the sphere, we will not see a shape rendered to the browser without a material and mesh.

Immediately beneath the line on which we created the cube's Phong material, write:

```
const sphereMaterial = new THREE.MeshLambertMaterial({
    color: 'tan'
});
```

The code to construct the sphere's material is nearly identical to the code we used to construct the cube's material. Instead of Phong shading, however, which emphasizes the specular glare, or shininess, of an object, we wrap the sphere in a Lambert material, which creates a dull, muted, diffuse appearance on an object.

Mesh = Material + Geometry

To see the effect of the material in our scene, let's complete the process of creating the sphere's mesh, positioning it, and adding it to our scene data structure.

Beneath the instantiation of the cube mesh in the MESHES section of the main function, write:

```
const sphere = new THREE.Mesh(sphereGeometry, sphereMaterial);
sphere.position.set(-sphereRadius - 1, sphereRadius + 2, 0);
scene.add(sphere);
```

Here, again, we apply the same creation pattern to the sphere object as we did the cube, defining its position as a function of its size. You may change the value of the sphereRadius variable in the sphere's geometry constructor to see how the edit impacts its position. Saving and loading the scene will render a tan sphere to the left of our rotating cube, with its bottom half in shadow.

Let's rotate the sphere as we did the cube, to better see the impact Lambert material has on the scene's light model. Inside the draw function, add:

```
sphere.rotation.x += 0.01;
sphere.rotation.y += 0.01;
sphere.rotation.y += 0.01;
```

Saving and loading the scene renders the sphere still half in shadow. However, depending on the resolution of your browser and the brightness of your monitor, you may notice that the sphere displays a dull, matte quality to its tan color as it rotates beneath the directional light. Changing the sphere's material from Lambert to Phong, like the material used on the cube, saving, and reloading the scene will hopefully make clear the distinction between the diffuse and specular qualities of Lambert and Phong materials, respectively.

LAMBERT AND PHONG SHADERS

Lambert is a shading model that calculates the reflection of light from an object's vertices. The quality of lighting is diffuse and will not change depending on the position of the camera or viewer. Therefore, the diffuse light value of a material can be calculated and set once during an application's runtime.

Phong shading, on the other hand, is a lighting equation calculated at each pixel an object occupies on a screen. The quality of Phong lighting is shiny, specular, resulting in highlights. The calculation of a Phong material's specular value is entirely dependent on the position of the camera, or viewer. Because the Phong lighting model requires recalibration for every transformation of the camera's position, the renderer calculates its value each frame, resulting in a heavier computational toll.

The quality of light's reflection from a material is not the only property we can manipulate to add realness to our WebGL scenes. In addition to colors, material objects in Three.js also offer the option to add textures to subjects, which add detail to the scene.

Textures

In 3D graphics a texture is an image file the graphics pipeline applies to a material. As lighting can become an expensive operation in the construction of a 3D scene, XR developers use images to add fidelity to a scene at low cost.

UV Maps

One example of a texture is a UV map (Figure 5-2), which applies an image to an object as if the image were wallpaper or gift wrap. The U in the name UV refers to the point on the texel, texture pixel, that maps to the x coordinate of a mesh; the V refers to the y coordinate. Mapping U to x and V to y allows a shader to properly wrap a material around a mesh according to instruction.

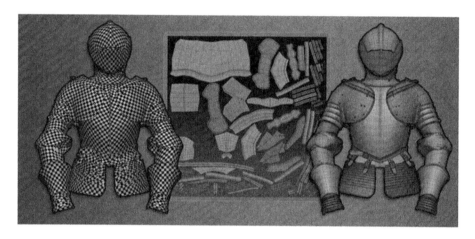

Figure 5-2. *UV maps are image files that associate a point on a mesh with a point on a texture. The one-to-one relationship allows for convenient storage of a texture and easy wrapping around a model*

Another example of a texture is a normal map, which alters the normal vectors of an object's surface and in turn impacts the output of the lighting model.

Normal Maps

A normal vector is a vector perpendicular to the surface of a mesh at a given point. The angle between a pixel's normal vector and reflecting light informs the value of light received by the camera. Altering the orientation of a surface's normal vector will change the angle of the surface's reflection, affecting the path traveled by the light ray en route to the camera.

Continuing with this chapter's exercise, we will add a normal map to the sphere, a plane geometry to the scene to mimic the ground, and both a UV and normal map to the plane to better simulate a landscape.

Three.js TextureLoader

To add an image texture to our Three.js scene, however, we must first create an instance of a Three.js TextureLoader object.

Beneath the MATERIALS header in the JavaScript file for this exercise, create a constant variable called textureLoader.

```
const textureLoader = new THREE.TextureLoader();
```

To load a texture into a Three.js scene, we call the load() function on the TextureLoader instance in our script and pass into it the relative file path location of the image file we'd like to use as a texture. You can find the image files I use for this example in the course files for the chapter. The source code for this book is available on GitHub via the book's product page, located at www.apress.com/9781484263174.

As we will soon add a geometric plane object to our scene to serve as the ground, let's load an image texture of small rocks and pebbles.

```
const planeTextureMap = textureLoader.load('textures/pebbles.jpg');
```

For convenience sake, I have created a folder called textures in the root of my project. If you choose to store your image file at a different file path, then be sure to point the loader to its location using the file path relative to where you've saved the main HTML document for the exercise. For an example of the folder structure I've used in the creation of the exercise, refer to the exercise's GitHub page in the course materials.

Of course, to use a texture in our scene, we first need a geometry around which to wrap it.

Texture as a Property of Material

In the GEOMETRY section of the JS file, below the code blocks in which you created the cube and sphere objects, define the width and height values for the plane object.

```
// Create the upright plane
const planeWidth = 256;
const planeHeight =  128;
```

With the dimensions of the plane defined, we can pass them into the Three.js `PlaneGeometry()` constructor, as we similarly did for the creation of both the cube and sphere.

```
const planeGeometry = new THREE.PlaneGeometry(
    planeWidth,
    planeHeight
);
```

In the MATERIALS section of the file, immediately beneath the line on which we declared the `planeTextureMap` variable, save the output of the `Three.MeshLambert()` constructor to a constant variable, and set the map property of the material to the texture map we loaded using JavaScript object notation.

```
const planeMaterial = new THREE.MeshLambertMaterial({
    map: planeTextureMap
});
```

Recall that some constructors in Three.js, such as those for materials, accept anonymous JavaScript objects as parameters. The map property is a built-in property of the Material class provided by Three.js. Using a colon after the property's name assigns the proceeding variable as a value to the property.

Texture ➤ Material ➤ Geometry ➤ Mesh

Following the same protocol we used for both the cube and sphere objects, we complete the creation of the plane in our scene by creating a mesh that unites the vertices and material of our plane.

In the MESHES section of the JS file, beneath the instantiation of the sphere mesh, add the code:

```
const plane = new THREE.Mesh(planeGeometry, planeMaterial);
scene.add(plane);
```

Save and load the scene through your local Web server into the browser window.

Again, nothing appears to have happened in the scene. Yet, no errors appear in the console; we've written our code properly. What, then, has happened?

The Lighting Model

By default, Three.js instantiates a plane with a 90-degree orientation, perpendicular to the x-axis. The light model of a Three.js scene calculates the interaction between a light source and a material target to generate the values rendered to pixels on the screen. If the light in a scene does not hit a material, then the material and the object it wraps will not appear on screen.

Because the directional light we added to our scene in Part 1 of this exercise shines toward the negative y-axis from the position (0, 1, 0) by default, the rays emitted from the directional light run parallel to the surface texture of the plane (Figure 5-3). Parallel lines, of course, never intersect[3]; the directional light in our scene never touches the surface of our vertical plane.

---

[3]In Euclidean geometry. "An Ancient Theorem and a Modern Question." In Roger Penrose, *The Road to Reality: a Complete Guide to the Laws of the Universe* (Vintage Digital, 2016), pp. 31–37.

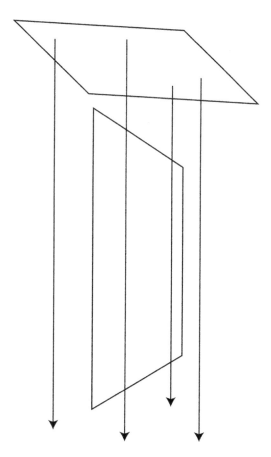

Figure 5-3. *Rays from a directional light travel at a perpendicular angle to the source. If the target's surface is also perpendicular to the source, then the rays and the surface will not intersect*

Light Position

To better demonstrate the situation, let's move the directional light in our scene to shine onto the plane material texture we've added.

We can accomplish this task by setting the position property of the light object to a desired Vector3 position, as we have done with the cube and sphere objects, beneath the code that instantiates it.

```
const light = new THREE.DirectionalLight(color, intensity);
light.position.set(0, 30, 30);
scene.add(light);
```

The vector sent as a parameter to the light position's set function places the light 30 clicks up the y-axis and 30 clicks from the origin along the z-axis, like the camera.[4] However, the directional light still shines downward; its rays still travel parallel to the vertical plane in our scene.

Light Target

To tilt the angle of the light's projection, we can set the directional light's built-in target property, provided by Three.js, to the plane object in our scene.

Following the addition of the light object to the scene, write the code:

```
light.target = plane;
scene.add(light.target);
```

Adding the plane to the scene as the source of the `light.target` property removes the need to add the plane object to the scene directly. You can now delete the code that adds the plane to the scene following the instantiation of the plane's mesh. Saving and reloading the scene will reveal the vertical plane illuminated by the altered directional light (Figure 5-4).

---

[4]Three.js uses the SI units of measurement in which 1 Three.js unit is 1 meter. See the Three.js GitHub issue for more details. `https://github.com/mrdoob/three.js/issues/6259`

Figure 5-4. *Moving and tilting the directional light in the scene creates an oblique angle between the light's rays and the texture map, revealing the texture's image*

Of course, the ground in our scene cannot realistically stand perpendicular to the camera's lens. To correct the irregularity, we can write code to rotate our plane 90 degrees using the radian values of the unit circle, which we learned in an earlier chapter (Figure 5-5).

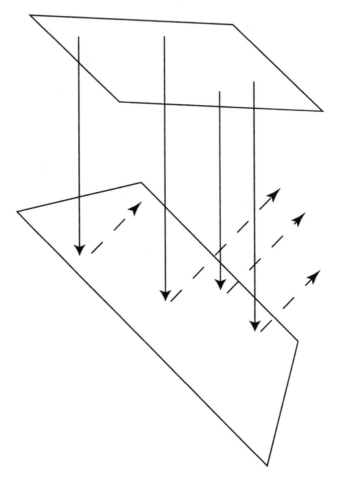

Figure 5-5. *Rotating the angle of the plane geometry 90 degrees from its original position allows the surface of the texture map to intersect the rays of the directional light*

Light Rotation

As the unit circle measures a 180-degree rotation with the value Pi, we can define a 90-degree rotation as Pi / 2 around the x-axis.

```
const plane = new THREE.Mesh(planeGeometry, planeMaterial);
plane.rotation.x = Math.PI / 2;
scene.add(plane);
```

Saving and loading the scene will still not render the plane as we'd hope; however, we have rotated the plane face down.

The Material Side Property

To ensure the plane's texture appears in the WebGL context, we can set the side property of the `planeMaterial` to the built-in Three.js value `DoubleSide`.

In the anonymous JS object we passed into the plane's `LambertMaterial` constructor, set the value of the side property.

```
const planeMaterial = new THREE.MeshLambertMaterial({
    map: planeTextureMap,
    side: THREE.DoubleSide
});
```

Saving and loading the scene in the browser will finally show the plane wrapped in its texture as the ground beneath the rotating shapes (Figure 5-6).

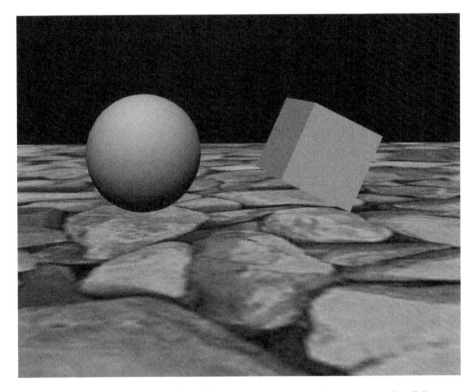

Figure 5-6. *Reorienting the plane geometry 90 degrees and adding the* DoubleSide *property to the material creates the illusion of the ground*

As demonstrated in Part 2 of this exercise, creating convincing XR scenes for the Web often requires more than just the placement of geometry in a three-dimensional space. Because the goal of XR applications is immersion for the user, tools that provide color, light, and texture to a scene are essential components of the XR developer's toolkit. Fortunately, Three.js provides convenient abstractions above the WebGL API to simplify the addition of materials, lights, and image textures to an XR scene.

Part 2 Recap

- Added a plane and sphere object to the scene through their respective geometry constructors

- Added materials to the objects

- Created a texture-loading object to handle uploading image texture files

- Applied textures to materials

- Learned how translating and rotating lights and objects impacts the lighting value calculated from materials

Exercise 4, Part 3: Fog, Backgrounds, Ambient Lights, and Normal Maps

In addition to the fundamental principles of geometry, materials, lighting, and textures, convincing 3D XR experiences include more nuanced management of a scene's appearance. While much of the reality of an XR scene can originate from high-quality, artfully rendered models, Three.js offers convenient access to basic tools that can elevate the fidelity of an XR scene. In Part 3 of this chapter's exercise, we will explore methods of finely tuning the appearance of a scene in Three.js. By the end of the exercise, you will have a more complete understanding of how the lighting model in Three.js, and WebGL in general, creates the illusion of reality through mathematical manipulation of the relationship between materials and lights. In this part of the exercise you will:

- Change the background color of a scene

- Learn the role fog plays in 3D scenes and how to create it

- Complement a directional light with an ambient light object

- Apply normal maps to materials to create the illusion of a nonuniform surface

- Learn the meaning of terms like mipmapping and anisotropy in application to the filtering of image textures to increase a scene's fidelity and performance

- Animate properties of objects in a scene through the creation of parametric equations

Scene Background

Changing the color of a scene's background in Three.js is a straightforward task. The Three.js Scene object includes a property, conveniently, called background. Setting the value of this property to a normalized RGB value applies the color to the background of the scene.

Below the line on which we instantiated the scene in our JS file, set the scene's background property to a light blue, or any other color you'd like.

```
// create the scene
const scene = new THREE.Scene();
scene.background = new THREE.Color(0.3, 0.5, 0.8);
```

The Scene object in Three.js also provides a public property called fog.

Fog

Fog is a feature that graphics-rendering hardware can produce with relative ease. To take advantage of the trait, we can instantiate a new Three.js fog object and set it equal to the scene's fog property, as we did with its background property.

Beneath the code written to set the background color, create a constant variable called fog and set it as the target variable for a new fog object. Then set the newly created fog object as the source for the scene's fog property.

```
const fog = new THREE.Fog("gray", 1, 100);
scene.fog = fog;
```

The parameters of the fog constructor are a color, a near, and a far value. The renderer uses the near and far values to calculate the linear gradation of the fog. The smaller the difference between the two values, the thicker the fog rendered. One reason computer graphics artists render fog into a scene is because the fog reduces the computation required to calculate visual fidelity. After saving and loading the scene, you should see a blue background, like a sky, with an amount of gray fog varying into the background (Figure 5-7).

Figure 5-7. *A Three.js scene object has a property that allows for the creation of fog*

As the scene is now, the diffuse Lambert material on the sphere doesn't demonstrate the rotation of the object enough for my taste. One way to emphasize the rotation of an object is to include a texture map that influences the object's interaction with a light source. In the graphics rendering pipeline, a texture that achieves such a result is called a normal map.

Applying a Normal Map

A normal map is an image file that stores information other than color as its values. The information a normal map stores is a vector that reflects light at uneven angles. The result is a texture that appears to have bumps and ridges. Yet, a normal map does not change the geometry of a shape; it only changes the appearance of the shape's geometry. To see the normal map in practice, we will add one to the sphere object in our scene.

If you are following along with the steps in this exercise, then you can find the sphere normal map I am using in the course files on GitHub, accessible through the book's product page at www.apress. com/9781484263174. Whichever normal map you choose to use, save it in the texture's folder of your project. As it was with the texture map for the plane mesh, the textureLoader in our scene requires a relative location path for the normal map file.

In the MATERIALS section of the JS file, either above or below the code defining the plane's texture map, load and create the sphere's material and normal map as follows:

```
const sphereNormalMap = textureLoader.load('textures/
sphere_normal.png');
sphereNormalMap.wrapS = THREE.RepeatWrapping;
sphereNormalMap.wrapT = THREE.RepeatWrapping;
const sphereMaterial = new THREE.MeshStandardMaterial({
    color: 'tan',
    normalMap: sphereNormalMap
});
```

Take care to note that instead of the Lambert material, we use the Three.js class `MeshStandardMaterial` to hold a reference to our sphere's normal map.

Physically Based Materials

A standard material in Three.js refers to a physically based rendering model that calculates a more complex equation than either Lambert or Phong materials. The model is called physically based because it recreates the manner in which light behaves in the real world, while Lambert and Phong equations only seek to simulate it.

Saving and loading the scene shows a textured sphere whose rotation appears more clearly because of the manner in which the grooves on its surface reflect the rays of the directional light (Figure 5-8). However, while the sphere looks more realistic, the texture map of the plane stands out as synthetic in contrast.

Figure 5-8. *A normal map texture on the Three.js standard material surrounding the sphere's mesh object creates the illusion of a rough surface without changing the shape's geometry*

Wrapping

One reason the texture map of the plane appears fake is its relative size to the sphere. We can reduce the size of the pebbles in our texture map by shrinking the image and repeating it across the surface of our plane.

Between the lines on which we loaded the plane's texture map and created its material, set the repeating and wrapping properties of the texture.

```
const planeTextureMap = textureLoader.load('textures/pebbles.jpg');
    planeTextureMap.wrapS = THREE.RepeatWrapping;
    planeTextureMap.wrapT = THREE.RepeatWrapping;
    planeTextureMap.repeat.set(16, 16);
    const planeMaterial = new THREE.MeshLambertMaterial({...
```

Setting the image to repeat every 16 pixels in both the width (S and/or U) and height (T and/or V) directions is a technique known as tiling, as the function reduces the image to a 16×16 sample like a tile in a mosaic. Textures in Three.js have different wrapping properties. The RepeatWrapping property lays the sampled image tile side by side until covering the desired surface. You can find definitions for other types of wrapping options on the Three.js documentation website.

SAMPLING AND THE POWERS OF 2

One noteworthy feature about WebGL is that its image sampling limits the dimensions of tiles to powers of 2, such as 2, 4, 8, 16, 64, etc. The dimensions need not be equal, but both must be a power of 2. See the Three.js documentation and/or WebGL specification for more information.

Applying the changes from the previous step to the scene produces an image such as one seen in Figure 5-9.

Figure 5-9. *Sampling the texture map of the plane geometry creates a tiling pattern that better reflects reality*

While the pebbles appear more realistic in size, the manner in which they fall off in focus stretches credibility. To better represent the way surfaces appear to extend into the distance, Three.js offers several solutions. We will use two of them in the steps to follow.

Mipmapping

One technique 3D artists employ to recreate the illusion of a texture's depth is called mipmapping. A mipmap is a hierarchical data structure of an image sampled at increasingly smaller values. Metaphorically, a mipmap is like a pyramid, the top of which represents the smallest sampled resolution. The base of the mipmap pyramid is the sample of the image with the highest resolution. In a WebGL application, the renderer will select which sample of the image, or layer of the mipmap pyramid, to draw as a function of the distance to the camera.

The theory behind mipmapping addresses problems that arise from aliasing, which is the distortion created when a fragment color occupies only a portion of a screen's pixel. The further the UV coordinate of a texture lies from the camera in screen space, the smaller the image the renderer will select to paint. Conversely, UV texture coordinates that appear closer to the camera are rendered using the higher resolution image, because it is more likely for an image to fill more pixels as its proximity to a scene's camera increases. As is its way, Three.js offers a convenient abstraction for the creation of a mipmap data structure. Though the use of mipmaps is obviously enabled, Three.js also provides built-in functions that simulate the effect of mipmaps.

To implement an example of a mipmap filter on the map texture of the ground plane in our scene, set the property of the texture's `minFilter` above the plane's Lambert Mesh declaration.

```
planeTextureMap.minFilter = THREE.NearestFilter;
```

The Three.js class `NearestFilter` refers to a built-in constant offered by the library that calculates the value of a texel, or texture-portraying pixel, from the texture's closest UV coordinate. Applying the `minFilter` to the plane's texture map creates a surface image that extends into the scene's z-axis more realistically.

Anisotropy

In real everyday life, however, textures and surfaces don't only shrink in size with distance, they also appear to blur. Computer graphics cards recreate this physical trait artificially with a function that calculates an image's property called anisotropy. In 3D graphics, anisotropy refers to the property of an image on screen that warps in accordance with the angle of view. To see it in practice is to better understand its application.

Set the plane texture map's anisotropy property to the value of the function gl.getMaxAnisotropy(), where gl is the variable of the WebGLRendering context.

```
planeTextureMap.anisotropy = gl.getMaxAnisotropy();
```

The getMaxAnisotropy() function on the Three.js renderer object calculates the maximum level of anisotropy offered by a system's hardware. Alternating between the minFilter and anisotropy properties by commenting out one, running the scene, then commenting out the other will provide you with an intuitive, visual understanding of how the tools may fit into your preferred aesthetic.

While tiling and applying anisotropic filters to a texture lend believability to a scene, an image, by its nature, exists in two dimensions; there is no height, for example (Figure 5-10). To add a bit more detail to the surface of our plane, we can apply a normal map texture to the plane's material, as we did with the sphere object in our scene.

Figure 5-10. *The tiled texture of the plane's texture map appears flat without a normal map applied*

Normal Mapping the Plane

You can find the plane normal map I use in this exercise in the chapter files for the course located at www.apress.com/9781484263174.

Create a variable to hold the normal map exported by the textureLoader object. Set the wrap, minification, and tiling properties as you did for the sphere's normal map in Step 3. Change the type of material from Lambert to Standard, too.

```
const planeNorm = textureLoader.load('textures/pebbles_
normal.png');
planeNorm.wrapS = THREE.RepeatWrapping;
```

```
planeNorm.wrapT = THREE.RepeatWrapping;
planeNorm.minFilter = THREE.NearestFilter;
planeNorm.repeat.set(16, 16);
const planeMaterial = new THREE.MeshStandardMaterial({
    map: planeTextureMap,
    side: THREE.DoubleSide,
    normalMap: planeNorm
});
```

A close-up of the plane's surface texture in Figure 5-11 demonstrates the effect created by the application of a normal map texture to a standard material in Three.js.

Figure 5-11. *Applying a normal map to a texture beneath a light can create the illusion of shadows, with low cost to the GPU*

Ambient Light

Another option Three.js provides to supplement the reality of a scene is the ambient light object. Unlike directional lights in Three.js, an ambient light object computes the value of a pixel as a product of both direct and reflected light. The application of ambient light to a scene creates a lighting model that more closely resembles the physical property of light, bounce, and reflection. For example, turning on a lamp in a bedroom will not only illuminate objects directly in the path of the rays emitted from the lamp. Light bouncing and reflecting off surfaces in the room will contribute to the bedroom's overall quality of light. While the overall level of light, or brightness, in the room may rise, the color value of surfaces will change also, as light reflected from surfaces may change the composition of its original wavelengths. The product of a lighting model that considers directional and ambient light, therefore, may lend degrees of fidelity to a Three.js scene.

To add an ambient light to our project, write the following code beneath the lines on which you added the directional light to the scene.

```
const ambientColor = 0xffffff;
const ambientIntensity = 0.2;
const ambientLight = new THREE.AmbientLight(ambientColor,
ambientIntensity);
scene.add(ambientLight);
```

Like the directional light, the ambient light constructor accepts a color and normalized intensity value as arguments. While I set the color of the ambient light to the same value as the directional light, you can experiment with the impact different hexadecimal color values have on the overall lighting of the scene.

Animation with Parametric Equations

As the final steps in this chapter's exercise, we will animate the rotation of the directional light around the objects in our scene to fully understand the influence of normal map textures in the lighting model for a scene.

Functions of Time

Parametric equations are equations that output x,y values as a function of time. Creative coding relies heavily on the use of parametric equations to compute and animate geometric behaviors for shapes and lights. To demonstrate the behavior of normal maps on geometric shapes in a scene, we will animate the directional light in our scene to move around the scene as if in orbit. To accomplish this requires two steps: defining the equations and creating a variable for time.

Trigonometric Equations

Because we want the light to rotate around our scene as if traveling the path of a circle, we can leverage the consistency of cosine and sine waves.

Inside the `draw()` function, above the render call on the `gl` object, set the x and y values of the directional light object to the output of a cosine and sine curve, respectively, as a function of time.

```
light.position.x = 20*Math.cos(time);
light.position.y = 20*Math.sin(time);
gl.render(scene, camera);
```

Saving and running the scene now would render only black to the canvas because we have not yet defined the value of the variable time inside our `draw()` function.

Saving Time

As the application calls the `draw()` function as a callback inside the `requestAnimationFrame()` render loop, the timestamp of the scene passes implicitly into the function as a feature of the browser.

To leverage the default behavior of the browser's animation cycle, we capture the time value as a parameter inside the draw function and convert it from milliseconds to seconds using multiplication.

```
// DRAW
function draw(time){
    time *= 0.001;
...
```

Saving and rendering the scene in a Web browser through a local development server will depict the impact of the parametric functions on the position of the directional light.

As the function of a normal map is to reflect and reorient the rays of light received by a texture, both the sphere and plane objects in the scene show shadows that rise and fall in intensity on the surfaces of these textures. Remember that we have not changed the geometry of the shapes, at all. The deformities, ridges, and dimples on the objects are only mathematical constructs computed by the shaders on the graphics hardware of your machine. The value of tools such as normal maps in XR scenes is not only in the quality of their appearance, but also in their minimal impact on performance. Savvy applications of textures and materials in Three.js can transform the atmosphere of scenes without requiring high computational cost.

Part 3 Recap

- Changed the background color property of a scene object

- Added fog to a scene and learned how to change its saturation

- Added an ambient light object to complement the scene's directional light

- Applied normal mapping textures to materials to simulate the interaction between materials and light

- Applied minification and anisotropic filters to an image texture to increase the fidelity and performance of a scene

- Created parametric equations in the animation loop that changed the property of an object in the scene over time

Summary

The purpose of this chapter has been to highlight few of the many ways Three.js abstracts the complexity of WebGL. For example, through providing constructor functions for primitive shapes like boxes, spheres, and planes Three.js removes the responsibility for creating attribute buffers of vertices from the shoulders of the developer. While Three.js may hide some of the deeper functionality of WebGL beneath user-friendly abstractions, it still allows for the experienced developer to dig into the library to create more complex effects. Because of its appeal to both novice and seasoned developers, Three.js has become a fundamental tool for the creation and design of WebXR experiences. In the following chapter we will use the scene we have created in Exercise 4 as an entree into implementing the WebXR API for a VR headset.

In this chapter you:

- Used Three.js primitive geometry constructors to place shapes, lights, and a camera in a Three.js scene

- Learned the distinction between materials in Three. js, including Lambert, Phong, and physically based rendering materials

- Covered the basics of lighting in a 3D scene, such as the flow of rays from a directional light, the cost efficiency of diffuse lighting, and the quality of specular highlights

- Created fog to add fidelity to a scene and spare computational cost for vertices in the distance

- Created a Three.js texture loader object to import image files from a local machine

- Applied image files as textures to materials on meshes to create different effects

- Used mipmap tiling and anisotropy functions built into Three.js to better render more realistic textures

- Learned the role normal maps play in the creation of shadows on the surfaces of shapes

- Used parametric equations, where x and y values are a function of time, to animate the constant motion of an object in a Three.js scene

CHAPTER 6

Entering VR Through WebXR

In the previous chapter we delved into the 3D JavaScript library built atop the WebGL API called Three.js. By building a scene with geometric primitives and textures, we saw the ease Three.js provides to WebXR developers; gone were the bare-bones data structures of attribute buffers and vertex arrays. However, while Three.js offers a convenient, high-level abstraction of WebGL functionality, it is still, at its core, no more than a rendering tool for the browser. While Three.js may help a developer paint a three-dimensional scene to a Web browser's HTML canvas element, it cannot, alone, pass that scene to a peripheral device such as a virtual reality headset. In this chapter we will use the Three.js scene we built in Exercise 4 of the previous lesson to launch an immersive WebXR session on an Oculus Quest VR headset. By the end of this chapter and its exercise, you will have an understanding of how the capabilities provided by the WebXR API cooperate with the rendering functionality built into Three.js.

In this chapter you will:

- Learn to use the USB debugging features of the Oculus Quest

- Access the debugging tools of the Oculus Quest through the Android Debug Bridge application

© Rakesh Baruah 2021
R. Baruah, *AR and VR Using the WebXR API*,
https://doi.org/10.1007/978-1-4842-6318-1_6

- Create an interface to connect the Quest and a local development server through the WebXR API

- Learn the value of Promises in JavaScript to handle asynchronous calls to Web services

- Learn the importance of scope and closure to creating XR sessions on the Web

- Use the browser's developer tools to forward the content from a host machine to a peripheral XR device

Setting Up the Debug Environment

Before we begin with the fun of creating a connection between our Three.js project and the WebXR API, we must first set up our tools for development. For this exercise, the tool we need is a peripheral device for which we have developer access and on which we can view immersive VR content. If you do not have access to a device capable of virtual reality, you will not be excluded. Searching the extensions offered by your browser provider, you will likely find a WebXR Emulator tool created by the team at Mozilla Mixed Reality.[1] Download the extension and review its documentation to better learn how to use the emulator in place of a physical device.

Debugging WebXR on an Oculus Quest

The following steps apply directly to connecting an Oculus Quest headset as a developer device through USB to a PC running Windows 10. Where appropriate, I've added footnotes for URLs that may host information helpful for case-specific troubleshooting.

---

[1]WebXR Emulator by Mozilla Mixed Reality: `https://blog.mozvr.com/webxr-emulator-extension/`

Android Debug Bridge (ADB) and the Oculus Mobile App

1. Download and install Android Studio

   a. Android Studio provides the software developer kit (SDK) required for debugging on the Oculus Quest.[2]

   b. Android Studio provides the ADB program, which facilitates communication between a computer and a connected Android device such as the Oculus Quest.[3]

2. Download the ADB software drivers required by the manufacturer of the Android device on which you want to test WebXR applications.

   a. ADB drivers for Windows 10 can be found at this link provided by Oculus.[4]

   b. Machines running Mac and Chrome OS do not require the download of additional drivers, according to official documentation.[5]

   c. Users operating on Linux machines should check the Android Studio documentation for the requirements of their systems.[6]

---

[2]Download Android Studio: `https://developer.android.com/studio`

[3]ADB and Quest: `https://developer.oculus.com/documentation/native/android/mobile-adb/`

[4]Oculus ADB drivers for Windows: `https://developer.oculus.com/downloads/package/oculus-adb-drivers/`

[5]Oculus device setup: `https://developer.oculus.com/documentation/native/android/mobile-device-setup/`

[6]Some users have struggled with USB debugging Oculus devices on platforms other than Windows. Helpful solutions may be found at this link from the XDA Developers website: `https://www.xda-developers.com/install-adb-windows-macos-linux/`

173

3. After downloading the ADB drivers for the Oculus Quest for Windows 10, navigate to the unzipped folder location and right-click install on the winusb. inf file.

   a. If you do not see the winusb.inf file in your unzipped folder, confirm that your file explorer has enabled the display of hidden files by clicking the View menu in the file explorer toolbar.

   b. For convenience, move these files to a folder you name ADB at the root location of the local hard drive (C:).

4. To enable debugging on the Quest through a computer, you must first download the Oculus app to your smartphone.

5. Once the app has downloaded, open it and sync it with your Oculus device.

6. In the settings beneath the synced device on the app, activate USB debugging.

7. Connect the Quest device to your computer using a USB-C to USB-3 cable.[7]

8. Navigate to the location of the SDK platform-tools folder installed by Android Studio.

   a. By default, on Windows 10, Android Studio saves the SDK/platform-tools folder in a directory located within Local Disk(C:) ➤ Users ➤ [your_username]➤ AppData ➤ Local ➤ Android ➤ SDK ➤ platform-tools.

---

[7]Quest devices also may connect to computers through the Oculus Link interface: https://support.oculus.com/394778968099974

9. Open a command prompt in the Windows Start menu by entering cmd into the Windows search bar (note: you may have to run as the administrator, depending on the setup of your account).

10. Navigate to the SDK/platform-tools folder by entering cd at the command prompt [copy/paste the location path to the platform-tools folder from File Explorer].

11. Once inside the platform-tools folder in your command prompt window, type adb devices.

12. If you have successfully installed Android Studio, the SDK, and the required ADB drivers for your device, such as the Quest, then ADB should begin running and display a list of Android devices connected to your machine.

13. If a device appears as unauthorized, then activate your device, like the Quest, and enable USB debugging when provided by the prompt.

    a. If you do not see the prompt inside your headset, then open and run the Oculus app on your computer.[8]

14. Reenter adb devices into the windows command prompt. If you have successfully enabled USB debugging on your Quest device through your computer, then the Android device previously listed will appear as authorized.

15. To confirm Windows 10 has installed the ADB driver required by Android Studio and the Oculus Quest,

---

[8]Download Oculus device software here: https://www.oculus.com/setup/

navigate to the Computer Manager application
through the Windows Start menu.

16. In Computer Manager, locate Device Manager ➤
     Portable Devices ➤ Quest [or the brand of your
     device]. Right-click the device and select Update
     driver.

17. Select `browse my computer` for driver software
     and search for drivers in the location where you
     saved the OEM ADB drivers from Oculus or another
     manufacturer.

     a. If you followed step 3.b, then this folder is C:\ADB\[device_
         driver_name]\usb_driver.

18. Select NEXT and confirm the MTP USB Device
     driver has been installed.

     a. If a driver other than the MTP USB Device driver appears,
         and your operating system has determined it is the best
         driver for the device attached, then either confirm the
         selection or refer to the documentation provided by the
         device manufacturer's website.

Upon completion of the aforementioned steps, you are now ready to
begin testing a WebXR application on your device.

Running a Demo from the Immersive Web

To see the WebXR API in action through our newly connected XR device,
let's access a sample project kindly provided to us by those responsible
for creating the WebXR API, the Immersive Web Working Group. The first
sample we will access is an immersive VR session. If your device is VR-
compatible, then follow along.

1. Make sure your device is not only connected to the Internet but also provides an application to browse the Web. For example, the Oculus Quest has a built-in browser accessible through its main menu toolbar.

2. After opening the browser in your XR device, navigate to the following URL, which is a page of WebXR samples accessible through the Immersive Web Working Group's GitHub repository: `https://immersive-web.github.io/webxr-samples/`.

3. Select the first sample listed on the page, "Immersive VR Session."

4. If your device and browser are capable of hosting an immersive VR session, you will see a large ENTER button near the top-left of the browsing window. In the browser inside your headset, select ENTER.

5. You should see a 360-degree model of the solar system, with a counter depicting your device's frames per a second.

If you have been able to experience the immersive VR scene created by the WebXR sample project, then you know your device and its browser are capable of viewing XR content through the WebXR API. Congratulations! Of course, this doesn't answer the question of whether or not our devices can access WebXR content we have developed on the local Web server inside our computers. That is what the next section of this chapter is about.

Preparing Our Scene for Immersive VR

Now that we've taken steps to enable debugging of XR applications on our machines through a connected XR device, we can finally turn our attention to transforming the Three.js scene we created in Exercise 4 into one we can experience in VR.

As the WebXR API is an implementation of a specification set forth by a group of XR industry leaders, it has norms that we, as responsible XR developers, should follow. The existence of these norms serves the interests of an end user's experience and security. Presumably, as a WebXR developer you'd like to create applications that people enjoy. To that end, the norms set forth by the Immersive Web Working Group serve the goals of both developers and users alike.

Life Cycle of a WebXR Application

The first important protocol laid out by the WebXR API is the life cycle of a VR application. The following are seven stages of an online VR app's life cycle, as laid out by the documentation on the Immersive Web Working Group's GitHub repository.[9]

1. **Query** to see if the desired XR mode is supported.

2. If support is available, **advertise XR functionality** to the user.

3. A user-activation event indicates that the user wishes to use XR.

4. **Request an immersive session** from the device.

---

[9]The Immersive Web Working Group on GitHub: `https://github.com/immersive-web/webxr`

5. Use the session to **run a render loop** that produces graphical frames to be displayed on the XR device.

6. Continue **producing frames** until the user indicates that they wish to exit XR mode.

7. **End the XR session**.

Before we begin adding WebXR functionality to the Three.js exercise we created in the last chapter, let's copy the index.html and index.js files and place them in a new folder that is a sibling to the old folder, a child of the same parent. Arranging the file structure of the exercise like this will allow us to access the Three.js module source files we imported during the exercise in Chapter 5.

As we've moved the location of our index.html file into a new folder, we must change the relative path of the Three.js import statement at the top of our index.js page. For both convenience and clarity, I will rename my index.js file for this exercise to index_xr.js and refer to it as such from now on.

There are four things we will address in Part 1 of this exercise:

1. We will reconfigure the declaration of some variables into the global scope.

2. We will define a VR button element that we will use to launch our XR application.

3. We will change the manner in which we created and defined the WebGL Rendering Context.

4. We will begin to divide the function we previously defined as main into two distinct functions, init() and animate().

Exercise 5, Part 1: Creating an XR Session Through the WebXR API

Stage 1 of the WebXR API instructs us to query if the user's Web browser supports the XR mode required by our application.

Stage 1: Is WebXR Supported?

As we want to test our Three.js scene in VR, the XR mode for which we'd like to query is "immersive-vr." The WebXR API includes language to query other modes, which we will address in later chapters. To query a browser's ability to display immersive-VR content, we can perform the following steps:

1. Create a new JS file called VRButton.js

2. Access the XR property of the browser's Navigator API

3. Asynchronously check if the browser supports WebXR

4. Accept the Promise returned from the XR object

5. Confirm the user's browser is secure

Create a New JS File Called VRButton.js

In the same folder for the HTML and index_xr.js files you created for this exercise, create a new JS file called VRButton.js.

Access the XR Object Through the Navigator API

The WebXR API provides a function we can use to check whether a browser supports the XR mode we'd like to request. To access functions provided by the WebXR API from our JavaScript files, we only need to access the XR object built into the navigator API[10] that a Web browser provides.

---

[10]The Navigator API on MDN: `https://developer.mozilla.org/en-US/docs/Web/API/Navigator`

1. In the VRButton.js file, create the following
    conditional block:

```
if (navigator.xr) {
    var button = document.createElement("button");
    navigator.xr.isSessionSupported('immersive-vr')
                .then(function(supported) {
                    if (supported) { EnterVR() }
                    else { NotFound(); }
    })...
```

The if statement checks if the browser's navigator property contains
an XR object. If it does, we instruct the Document object of the Web page
to create an HTML button element, which we save into a target variable
called button.

Send an Asynchronous Request

Next, we use dot notation to call the WebXR API's isSessionSupported()
function on the navigator's XR object. Because the XR mode for which
we'd like to test support is a VR session, we enter as an argument to the
isSessionSupported() function the string "immersive-vr," which is part of a
built-in enum data type provided by the WebXR API.[11]

You may not recognize the .then() function we call after the
isSessionSupported('immersive-vr') function. If you don't, then you're in
for quite a treat courtesy of the maintainers of the JavaScript language. The
.then() function is JavaScript syntax to handle an object called a Promise.
Like the keywords async and await, promises facilitate with the complexity
of asynchronous programming.

---

[11]List of XR session modes supported by WebXR API: `https://developer.`
`mozilla.org/en-US/docs/Web/API/XRSessionMode`

ASYNCHRONOUS PROGRAMMING

Asynchronous programming is a programming paradigm designed to handle the simultaneous requests and responses created by complex applications. One example of an asynchronous programming domain is a website's call to a database. As the response from a database located on a remote server may take some time, holding the processing of an app until the response arrives may impact performance. Tools such as JavaScript promises allow apps to send requests to databases or Web services, like the WebXR API, while continuing their execution while the request pends.

Receive the Returned Promise

In JavaScript, a promise is like a burrito; it's a package of nourishing bits wrapped for easy consumption. The contents of a promise burrito depend upon the function returning it. Because the WebXR API function isSessionSupported('immersive-vr') returns a Boolean value, one that is true if the browser supports VR and false if it does not, the innards of the promise burrito we receive in our .then() function are in the form of either a true or false Boolean value. If the burrito sent by the isSessionSupported('immersive-vr') function and received by its attached .then() function contains a true value, the .then() function executes the function within its parentheses.

If the XR object of the browser's navigator property does indeed support an immersive-VR mode, the .then() function executes the anonymous function we've defined inside its parentheses. The anonymous function takes the value wrapped inside the promise burrito, supported, as its argument, and it executes another conditional within its code block, specified by the opening and closing curly braces. The code we have written states that if the content of the promise burrito passed into the

.then() function is a true value, then our program should call a function we have yet to define called EnterVR().

Confirm the User's Browser is Secure

On the other hand, if the content of the promise burrito received by the .then() function is a false value, our program executes the NotFound() function inside the else clause. If the browser's navigator doesn't have an XR object, then the browser does not support the WebXR API.

1. We place the logic to handle this scenario in the else clause following the closing bracket of the if (navigator.xr) expression.

    ```
    ...} else {
        if (window.isSecureContext === false) {
            console.log('WebXR needs HTTPS');
        } else {
            console.log('WebXR not available');
        }
        return;
    }
    ```

    Inside the else clause we've written to handle a scenario in which a user's browser does not support the WebXR API, we define another conditional block. For security reasons, the WebXR specification requires that a WebXR session only launch in a secure browsing context, which browsers identify with the URL prefix "https."[12] Whether or not a browser supports a secure context is answered

---

[12]For more on secure browsing contexts, visit `https://developer.mozilla.org/en-US/docs/Web/Security/Secure_Contexts`.

by the isSecureContext property on the browser's global window object. As XR developers, we can avail ourselves of this information provided by the global window object to determine how to respond to a failed call to a browser's nonexistent XR object. If the navigator.xr object cannot be found for reasons pertaining to security, then we write to the browser's console that WebXR requires a secure browsing context. Else, we simply notify the user through the browser's console that their browser does not support functionality for the WebXR API.

If the user's browser does not support the WebXR API, or if their browsing context is not secure, then we have done all we can do for them. Unfortunately, they will not be able to experience our Three.js scene in VR.[13] However, if the user's browser has an XR object and supports the immersive-VR mode, then we must write the logic for the EnterVR() function we've called. Alternatively, if the user's browser has XR capabilities but has no connected device to support an immersive-vr session, then we must write the logic for the NotFound() function we've called. Let's begin by defining the logic for the NotFound() function, as that will be the easier of the two tasks.

2. In the VRButton.js document, above the if (navigator.xr) statement, define a new function called NotFound(). Enter the following code into the body of the NotFound() function.

---

[13]Hiding XR content from users is poor accessibility practice. All measures should be taken to create alternative content to serve all users.

```
function NotFound() {
    console.log('immersive-vr mode not found');
}
```

That's it! I told you it'd be easy. Now, let's move on to the more difficult task: writing the logic for the EnterVR() function.

3. Above the NotFound() function declaration, compose a new function with opening and closing brackets called function EnterVR().

```
function EnterVR() {

}
```

To determine what logic to place inside this function, let's refer to the second phase of a WebXR's life cycle as defined by the WebXR API.

Stage 2: Advertise XR Functionality to the User

The WebXR API defines phase 2 of a WebXR application's life cycle as one in which we, the developer, advertise XR functionality to the user. Because phase 3 of the XR app's life cycle requires a user-activation event to launch the XR application, we will present the user with a button to click if they'd like to enter an immersive-vr session.

1. Inside the EnterVR() function, write the following:

```
button.innerHTML = 'Enter XR';
var currentSession = null;
```

Recall that the button to which we refer, we created through a call to the Document object in step 1 of this exercise. With the button HTML element already created as a child of the Document object, we can manipulate the text it shows the user by setting its innerHTML property to 'Enter XR'. The innerHTML property is a built-in property provided by the HTMLElement interface, which our button, as an HTML element, inherits by default.

Why, though, do we create a new variable called currentSession and set it to null? The answer to that question has everything to do with Stage 3 of a WebXR's life cycle, as defined by the WebXR API.

Stage 3: Enable a User Activation Event

Stage 3 of the WebXR application's life cycle requires that we provide the user with the option to knowingly activate a WebXR session. We've provided a button for them to click, but we have not yet addressed what action our program will perform in response to a user's input. For that, we leverage yet another built-in feature of the Document Object Model API, the Event Handler.

Add an Event Handler to the Button

1. Below the code you wrote in the previous step, create an onclick event handler on the button object with an empty code block.

```
button.onclick = () => {

}
```

The arrow syntax following the declaration of the button's onclick event handler is an abbreviated way of creating an anonymous function in JavaScript. An equally valid way of defining the button's onclick event handler function would be:

```
button.onclick = function () {

}
```

Anonymous Functions

The preceding syntax is akin to the way we defined an anonymous function to handle the promise burrito received by the .then() function in step 2 of this exercise. However, in the service of brevity, JavaScript allows developers to define anonymous functions with an arrow (=>) in lieu of the function keyword. The empty parentheses preceding the arrow syntax simply illustrates that the anonymous function requires no arguments. Our .then() function from step 2 at least took a Boolean value as an argument to the anonymous function it called. With no argument provided to our button's onclick event handler's anonymous function, what then do we execute? As has been our practice in this exercise, let's return to the WebXR API's list of an XR application's life cycle.

Stage 4: Request an XR Session

As the fourth stage in an XR application's life cycle, the WebXR API instructs developers to request an immersive session from the user's device once the user has performed an action that demonstrates intention of launching an XR session. How do we request an XR session from a user's device?

Access WebXR Functions Through the XR Object

Fortunately, the designers of the WebXR API have provided us with another built-in function we can call on the browser's XR object.

1. Inside the empty code block of the button's onclick event handler, call the following built-in functions on the navigator's XR object:

```
navigator.xr
    .requestSession('immersive-vr', sessionInit)
    .then(onSessionStarted);
}
```

Like the xr.isSessionSupported() query from Stage 1, the XR object's built-in requestSession() function returns a Promise object. Because the requestSession() function returns a promise object, we can use the .then() function to catch the promise burrito returned by the call to requestSession(), as we did in step 2. However, unlike the promise burrito returned in step 2 of this exercise, the promise burrito returned by the xr.requestSession() function in this step wraps an XR session object, not a Boolean true,false value.

XR Session Object

The code we have written handles the XR session returned in the promise burrito by sending it directly to a function called onSessionStarted(), a function we have yet to define. Though we haven't yet defined the onSessionStarted() function in our VRButton.js document, writing it here reminds us of what information the logic of the function will have to handle. Before we can create the onSessionStarted() function, however, we must address the two parameters we have passed to the XR object's requestSession() function. The string value 'immersive-vr' we already know to be the mode of the XR session we are requesting. The second argument, sessionInit, however, is a variable we haven't even defined yet. What's going on?

Types of XR Modes

According to the WebXR API, the requestSession() function made available through the navigator's XR object accepts as parameters the mode of the XR session requested and features to implement upon an XR session's creation. The features requested can be either required or optional. The WebXR API allows the following features to be requested:

- Local

- Local-floor

- Bounded-floor

- Unbounded

Local refers to a stationary XR experience; local-floor defines a stationary XR experience that requires reference to a floor; bounded-floor means an XR experience should enable a user to move about a finite, defined space while wearing the XR device; and unbounded refers to a mobile XR experience that has no limitations to a user's movement.

Though the VR experience we've created in our Three.js scene does not require any movement from the user, let's define a sessionInit variable that holds a couple different optional features.

Initializing XR Session Features

1. Above the code written to request a session, define a sessionInit target variable and set its source value to a JavaScript object with the following key-value pair:

```
let sessionInit = {
    optionalFeatures: ["local-floor", "bounded-floor"]
};
```

Again, the names of both the key and value terms are provided by the WebXR API. Passing the JavaScript object to the XR object's requestSession() function as a parameter is a behavior predefined by the API's documentation.

Starting the XR Session

Now that we've requested an immersive-vr session with parameters defining optional features from the user's XR device, we have to determine how to handle the session returned within the Promise from the requestSession() function. In step 8 we used the .then() function to pass the contents of the promise burrito to a function called onSessionStarted. Let's write the logic of that function next.

1. Inside the body of the EnterVR() function, immediately below the initialization of the currentSession variable to null, write the stub of a function called onSessionStarted, which accepts as its parameter an XR session object.

    ```
    function onSessionStarted(session) {

    }
    ```

Recall that the onSessionStarted function is called by the onclick event handler attached to the button HTML element we have labeled "Enter XR." When the user visits the Web page for our application, our JavaScript will first query if their browser supports the functionality required by an immersive-vr XR session. If their browser supports the functionality, then our script creates an HTML button element to place on the Web page that instructs the user to press to launch our Three.js scene in VR. If the user clicks that button, our script fires an onclick event handler that, first, requests a session from the user's device. If the promise returned from the function contains an activated XR session, then our script passes the content of that promise, the XR session itself, to the function we have defined: onSessionStarted().

Stage 5: Run Render Loop

Stage 5 of the WebXR app's life cycle, as defined by the WebXR API, states that our onSessionStarted() function should run a render loop on our user's device. Fortunately, we've already created a render loop inside our Three.js scene through a call to setAnimationLoop() on our Three.js WebGLRenderer object instantiated in the main() function of our index.js script. Therefore, the logic of our onSessionStarted() function must, primarily, notify the Three.js WebGL Renderer defined in our main JavaScript file to ready itself for XR rendering. Hmm, but how can we access a JavaScript object we created in another file from our VRButton.js script? This, we will address in Part 2 of the exercise.

Part 1 Recap

- Created a VR Button JavaScript module

- Accessed the window's navigator API to query for an XR session

- Used a JavaScript promise to handle the response from the WebXR API Web service

- Requested an XR session with a parameter of optional features

- Created a button element to advertise XR content

- Attached an onclick event handler to the button to start and end an XR session

Exercise 5, Part 2: Scope, Closure, a Module, and a Singleton

The question of how to access the WebGL Rendering object from our main JS script inside our VRButton.js script is one seemingly easy to answer on its surface. For example, all we have to do is call the necessary function on the WebGL Renderer, which we saved in the target variable renderer in the index.js file in the previous chapter's exercise, right? Let's find out if this is the case together.

In Part 2 of this exercise you will:

- Learn about the WebXRManager object in Three.js

- Learn the importance of scope to a JS program

- Learn how to use closure in JS to sustain the state of an XR session

- Use the built-in functions of the three.js library to connect the Three.js rendering context to the XR session created through the WebXR API

WebXRManager in Three.js

First, we ask ourselves what function on the Three.js WebGL Rendering object, renderer, we must call to activate an XR rendering loop. A quick reference to the Three.js online documentation shows that the WebGL Rendering Object in Three.js has a property called xr, which in turn implements a Three.js interface called WebXRManager. After visiting the WebXRManager source code through the Three.js documentation, we learn that the WebXRManager interface provides a function conveniently called setSession(), which takes an XR session as an argument. Therefore, to connect the XR session we have requested in our VRButton.js script to the Three.js renderer on which we call our scene's animation loop in our main function, we need only use JavaScript's dot notation to access the setSession() function on our renderer object from within the VRButton.js script.

There is just one catch, though. While we aim to import our VRButton as a module into our main index JavaScript page, we do not have the ability to reach the Three.js renderer object from the code inside our VRButton.js script. The obstacle comes courtesy of a feature in JavaScript called scope.

Scope

Scope, in JavaScript, essentially refers to the accessibility of a variable from within the program of an application. For example, variables that we create inside functions cannot exist outside of their functions, unless we save them in other variables we either pass into the function or return from the function. Inadvertently, we've seen this principle at play in the previous exercise, in which we defined every new function within the curly braces of the main() function. If we had defined any functions outside the scope of the main function, then we would have had to take measures to pass variables required by both the main and additional functions back and forth as parameters and return values. While an approach like that is sound and effective, it does not make use of JavaScript's unique abilities.

Connecting the WebXRManager to an XR Session

To leverage the tools JavaScript inherently provides us as WebXR developers, we can place the Three.js WebGL Rendering object within the scope of our VRButton.js script by passing it as a parameter. To do so, we only need to perform two tasks: 1) we have to create a function in our VRButton script that accepts a Three.js rendering context as an argument, and 2) we have to make that function available to the scope in which the Three.js rendering object currently exists. Let's begin to solve this problem by completing the second task first.

Setup

At the beginning of this chapter I suggested that you copy the index.js file from the end of the exercise in Chapter 5 and rename it index_xr.js. I suggested the measure because in this section of the exercise we will apply some changes to the script. It will be best to retain an unaltered version of the JavaScript file to better understand the reasons behind the changes we will make.

Global Variables

1. First, we will define a slew of global variables just below the import statements at the top of the file.

    ```
    var gl, cube, sphere, light, camera, scene;
    ```

Once we create the variables at the top of the script's global scope, we no longer need the keywords const, let, or var to define the variables in the bodies of the function, as long as they too are in the global scope of the script.

Refactor

1. Second, we will break our main() function into two distinct functions called init() and animate(), which we will call just below the global declarations of our variables.

    ```
    init();
    animate();
    ```

Remove and Replace

1. Then, we will replace our main() function with separate functions beginning with the function called init(). Remove the declaration of the main function near the top of index_xr.js and replace it with the following function declaration:

```
function init() { ...
```

Though the content of the script will remain mostly the same as it was in its original version, I will represent it here for a bit more clarity in the context of our current lesson.

2. To that end, create the following headings using comment syntax within the init() function we renamed from main() in the previous step:

```
function init() {
    // create context
    // create camera
    // create the scene
    // GEOMETRY
    // create the cube
    // Create the Sphere
    // Create the upright plane
    // MATERIALS
    // MESHES
    //LIGHTS

}
```

The first significant change we will make to the init() function in index_ xr.js will be to the code we've used to define the WebGL Rendering context.

Enable the WebXRManager

Beneath the //create context comment inside the init() function, write the following code to create and define the Three.js WebGL Renderer, which we will pass as a parameter to a function inside VRButton.js.

```
// create context
gl = new THREE.WebGLRenderer({antialias: true});
gl.setPixelRatio(window.devicePixelRatio);
gl.setSize(window.innerWidth, window.innerHeight);
gl.outputEncoding = THREE.sRGBEncoding;
gl.xr.enabled = true;
document.body.appendChild(gl.domElement);
document.body.appendChild(VRButton.createButton(gl));
```

The setPixelRatio() and setSize() functions and the gl.outputEncoding property are not of great importance at this step of the exercise. Their roles pertain to the resolution of the scene. What is important in this step, however, is 1) the instantiation of the Three.js WebGL Renderer in the variable gl without a canvas object passed into the constructor; 2) the Boolean value true set to the property of the Three.js WebXRManager interface property called enabled; 3) the use of the DOM API function appendChild() to add the Three.js WebGL Renderer object's domElement property, which points to the HTML canvas element automatically created by the Three.js WebGLRenderer constructor, to the Web page's <body> section; and 4) the use of the DOM API to append the VR Button we created in VRButton.js to the Web page, while simultaneously calling a function that accepts the Three.js WebGL Renderer as an argument.

Though we have not yet written the logic within the createButton() function that the init() function calls in the script index_xr.js, we have at least defined the mechanism through which the XR session created by the WebXR API will connect to the render loop run on the Three.js renderer in our primary script called upon the launch of our Three.js scene.

While the remainder of the init() function is similar to the main() function it replaces in execution, you may prefer to copy the following code, which I've refactored for clarity.

```
import * as THREE from '../Threejs_Ex1/modules/three.module.js';
import {VRButton} from './VRButton.js';

var gl, cube, sphere, light, camera, scene;
init();
animate();

function init() {
    // create context
    gl = new THREE.WebGLRenderer({antialias: true});
    gl.setPixelRatio(window.devicePixelRatio);
    gl.setSize(window.innerWidth, window.innerHeight);
    gl.outputEncoding = THREE.sRGBEncoding;
    gl.xr.enabled = true;
    document.body.appendChild(gl.domElement);
    document.body.appendChild(VRButton.createButton(gl));

    // create camera
    const angleOfView = 55;
    const aspectRatio = window.innerWidth / window.innerHeight;
    const nearPlane = 0.1;
    const farPlane = 1000;
    camera = new THREE.PerspectiveCamera(
        angleOfView,
        aspectRatio,
```

```
    nearPlane,
    farPlane
);
camera.position.set(0, 8, 30);

// create the scene
scene = new THREE.Scene();
scene.background = new THREE.Color(0.3, 0.5, 0.8);
const fog = new THREE.Fog("grey", 1,90);
scene.fog = fog;

// GEOMETRY
// create the cube
const cubeSize = 4;
const cubeGeometry = new THREE.BoxGeometry(
    cubeSize,
    cubeSize,
    cubeSize
);

// Create the Sphere
const sphereRadius = 3;
const sphereWidthSegments = 32;
const sphereHeightSegments = 16;
const sphereGeometry = new THREE.SphereGeometry(
    sphereRadius,
    sphereWidthSegments,
    sphereHeightSegments
);

// Create the upright plane
const planeWidth = 256;
const planeHeight =  128;
```

```
const planeGeometry = new THREE.PlaneGeometry(
    planeWidth,
    planeHeight
);

// MATERIALS
const textureLoader = new THREE.TextureLoader();

const cubeMaterial = new THREE.MeshPhongMaterial({
    color: 'pink'
});

const sphereNormalMap = textureLoader.load('textures/
sphere_normal.png');
sphereNormalMap.wrapS = THREE.RepeatWrapping;
sphereNormalMap.wrapT = THREE.RepeatWrapping;
const sphereMaterial = new THREE.MeshStandardMaterial({
    color: 'tan',
    normalMap: sphereNormalMap
});

const planeTextureMap = textureLoader.load('textures/
pebbles.png');
planeTextureMap.wrapS = THREE.RepeatWrapping;
planeTextureMap.wrapT = THREE.RepeatWrapping;
planeTextureMap.repeat.set(16, 16);
planeTextureMap.minFilter = THREE.NearestFilter;
planeTextureMap.anisotropy = gl.getMaxAnisotropy();
const planeNorm = textureLoader.load('textures/pebbles_
normal.png');
planeNorm.wrapS = THREE.RepeatWrapping;
planeNorm.wrapT = THREE.RepeatWrapping;
planeNorm.minFilter = THREE.NearestFilter;
```

```
planeNorm.repeat.set(16, 16);
const planeMaterial = new THREE.MeshStandardMaterial({
    map: planeTextureMap,
    side: THREE.DoubleSide,
    normalMap: planeNorm
});

// MESHES
cube = new THREE.Mesh(cubeGeometry, cubeMaterial);
cube.position.set(cubeSize + 1, cubeSize + 1, 0);
scene.add(cube);

sphere = new THREE.Mesh(sphereGeometry, sphereMaterial);
sphere.position.set(-sphereRadius - 1, sphereRadius + 2, 0);
scene.add(sphere);

const plane = new THREE.Mesh(planeGeometry, planeMaterial);
plane.rotation.x = Math.PI / 2;

//LIGHTS
const color = 0xffffff;
const intensity = .7;
light = new THREE.DirectionalLight(color, intensity);
light.target = plane;
light.position.set(0, 30, 30);
scene.add(light);
scene.add(light.target);

const ambientColor = 0xffffff;
const ambientIntensity = 0.2;
const ambientLight = new THREE.AmbientLight(ambientColor,
ambientIntensity);
scene.add(ambientLight);
}
```

Now that we've addressed the problem of scope originally presented by the separation of our index_xr.js and VRButton.js scripts, we can turn our attention to that other pickle common in JavaScript: closure.

Closure

In JavaScript, the concepts of closure and scope go hand in hand. While scope refers to the life cycle of a variable in a JavaScript application, closure refers to the practice of leveraging the boundaries of scope to sustain the state of an object. The key fundamental to closure in JS is that functions in JS can exist as objects passed into other functions. Because functions manage the life cycles of variables within their curly braces, they maintain their scope no matter where they are called in an application. For example, if a variable dies upon the completion of its scope, and an XR session exists in our program as a variable, then how can we ensure the XR session runs without interruption?

Sharing the WebXRManager Between Scripts

One way we can reach this end is to invoke the life cycle of an XR session from within a function connected to the life cycle of the render loop in our Three.js scene. A very good example toward better understanding closure in JavaScript is to write the body of the createButton function we called in our revamp of the function recently renamed init(). By leveraging the closure provided by a module's function called as an argument passed into another function, we may run an XR session through the WebXR API and the render loop of our Three.js scene simultaneously.

The Singleton Design Pattern

Notice that in the second line of the index_xr.js script we added an import statement that imported {VRButton} from VRButton.js. The module paradigm in JavaScript allows us, developers, to move pieces of our code around an application for convenience and simplicity. The convenience arrives from not having to rewrite our code; the simplicity arrives from providing a single interface to all the functionality of another script. Closure emerges as a fortuitous byproduct of the module paradigm's separation of concerns. Encapsulating the functionality of a script in a singular JavaScript object is an example of the Singleton design pattern. To illustrate this phenomenon, let's reconfigure our VRButton.js script to better tailor it for the module we import into index_xr.js.

Storing Functionality in a Single Object

1. At the top of VRButton.js add a declaration for a variable called VRButton and set it equal to an empty JavaScript object.

```
var VRButton = {

}
```

The empty space between the opening and closing brackets of the VRButton target variable will become the entire script we export into index_xr.js. Most of the work we've already done, as what remains is primarily moving the logic we've written into the body of the JavaScript object VRButton defines. However, one important detail we have not yet addressed is the definition of the createButton() function we added to the body of our HTML document and called from init(). Because calling a function on an HTML element upon its addition to the Document object immediately invokes the function, it's imperative that we define the function first.

Storing a Function in a JS Object Property

1. Immediately within the opening curly brace of the VRButton target variable declaration, define a property called createButton and set its value to an anonymous function with two parameters.

```
var VRButton = {
    createButton: function(gl, options) {
        if (options && options.referenceSpaceType) {
            gl.xr.setReferenceSpaceType(options.
            referenceSpaceType);
        }
```

Remember that a JavaScript object can hold properties as key/value pairs. A colon indicates the name of a JS object's property to its left and the property's value to its right. We use the concept of anonymous functions in JS to immediately invoke the function upon a reference to the VRButton's createButton property. The parameters accepted by the anonymous function defined by the createButton property are gl and options, which we will connect with the Three.js renderer in our application and the optional settings of the XRSessionInit variable, which Three.js defaults to "local-floor".

2. Beneath the closing bracket of the if clause created above copy and paste the functions we've already created and defined in the VRButton.js document. These functions should include EnterVR(), function NotFound(), and the if/else conditional blocks that queried whether the navigator.xr object existed.

Now that we have a reference to our application's Three.js renderer available from within our VRButton.js script, we can easily connect the XR session created by the WebXR API's requestSession() function and passed as a resolved promise burrito to the function inside EnterVR() we've defined as onSessionStarted(session).

Connect the WebXRManager with the XR Session Loop

1. In the body of the OnSessionStarted() function, add the following code:

```
function onSessionStarted(session) {
    session.addEventListener('end', onSessionEnded);
    gl.xr.setSession(session);
    button.textContent = 'Exit XR';
    currentSession = session;
}
```

The first line of the function's body, session.addEventListener(), comes courtesy of the WebXR specification, which informs developers that in the interest of user experience, developers should instantiate an XR session already equipped with a mechanism to terminate itself upon a user's request.

The second line is the one that has eluded us and is the secret ingredient to launching our Three.js scene in accordance with the life cycle phases laid out by the WebXR API. Because we are encouraged to withhold the launch of an XR session until explicitly notified by the user through the click of a button on the Web page, we must connect the render loop on our Three.js renderer defined and called in index_xr.js with the XR session returned by the WebXR's requestSession() method fired by the VR button element's onclick event handler. We can finally fulfill this requirement by accessing the WebXRManager interface provided by the gl object, which serves as a proxy to the Three.js renderer instantiated in our init() function.

Referencing the Three.js renderer through the variable gl, which points to the object passed into the anonymous function stored in the createButton key, successfully overcomes the limitation created by JavaScript's treatment of variables in and out of scope.

Closure Sustains State

Most importantly, however, setting the source of the Three.js renderer's session to the session created inside the VRButton.js script allows us to apply the power of closure to sustain the state of the XR session. As we invoke the creation of the button object (with its quivering, waiting onclick handler ready to leap into action) near the top of our init() function in index_xr.js, we have guaranteed that the scope of the XR session, upon request, will endure through the existence of our animation loop.

Adding/Removing Event Listeners

Finally, the onSessionStarted() function replaces the text of the button element from "Enter XR" to "Exit XR" and sets the value of the variable currentSession, previously null, to the session initiated by the call to the WebXR API's requestSession() function.

Naturally, as we've created an onSessionStarted() function to handle the creation of an XR session, we should also create a function to handle the destruction of an XR session.

1. Beneath the closing bracket of the onSessionStarted() function, define a function called onSessionEnded.

```
function onSessionEnded() {
    currentSession.removeEventListener('end',
    onSessionEnded);
    button.textContent = 'Enter XR';
    currentSession = null;
}
```

Appropriately, the logic within the OnSessionEnded() body reverses the logic of its sibling function, onSessionStarted(). It removes the event listener from the currentSession object, restores the text of the button element, and resets the value of the variable currentSession to null.

To better understand the reason behind setting the value of currentSession to null upon a session's end, refer to step 6 of Part 1 of this exercise. In that step we initialized the currentSession value to null. Yet, we set the value of currentSession to the XR session created by the WebXR API inside the onSessionStarted() function. If we reset its value to null upon the calling of the end event on the XR session, then what purpose have we served by instantiating the currentSession variable with a null value?

In step 7 of Part 1 of this exercise, we created an onclick event handler on the button element. In step 9, inside the body of the anonymous function we set to fire upon the user's click of the button on the Web page, we defined the optional features of the XR sessionInit variable and requested an immersive-vr session via the XR object and WebXR API. Yet there is one scenario the logic we implemented does not address. What happens if a user clicks the "Exit XR" button on our Web page?

As our onclick button event handler is written now, the browser will attempt to request a second immersive-vr XR session. As a WebGL rendering context cannot host more than one XR session, our XR application will at best crash and at worst lock our user into a never-ending loop. To prevent both outcomes, we can use the value of the currentSession variable as a flag to indicate whether the application should request an XR session or not.

2. To add this feature to our application, we introduce an if/else conditional clause into the body of our onclick handler's anonymous function.

```
button.onclick = () => {
    if (currentSession === null) {
        let sessionInit = {
            optionalFeatures: ["local-floor",
            "bounded-floor"]
        };
    navigator.xr
            .requestSession('immersive-vr', sessionInit)
            .then(onSessionStarted);
    }
    else {
        currentSession.end();
    }
}
```

With the onclick handler redefined, our application now contains logic to request a new XR session *only* *if* one does not currently exist, and to otherwise call the end() function built into an XR session object provided by the WebXR API.

With the completion of the onclick handler for our VR Button, all that remains for us to do is to export the VRButton.js script's functionality as an object that the index_xr.js script can import.

3. To export the functionality of the VRButton object created in the VRButton.js script, simply add the following code to the end of the VRButton.js script, outside the final bracket that marks the closing of the VRButton object.

```
export {VRButton};
```

With the VRButton set to export and the index_xr.js script included with the ability to import the button and its functionality, we are almost ready to test our Three.js scene using the WebXR API.

Part 2 Recap

- Refactored the index.js file we created in the previous chapter to better suit the demands of the WebXR API

- Leveraged the idea of closure in JS to launch a function and its scope upon the creation of an HTML button

- Used the singleton pattern with a JS module to pass a WebGL Rendering object into the function that launched the XR session

Exercise 5, Part 3: The Homestretch

What remains to complete our application is the second function we defined at the top of our newly revamped index_xr.js page. We have initialized our scene and connected it to the creation of an XR session to reach the screen of a connected VR device. Now, we must write the logic required to run the render loop in Three.js.

In Part 3 of this exercise you will:

- Refactor the requestAnimationFrame() function from the previous exercise into a Three.js-specific call better suited for the WebXR API

- Reapply the render and resize functions to fit into the flow of the reformatted index_xr.js file

- Use browser developer tools to forward the port on which the local development server hosts the Three.js scene to a connected VR device

At the top of the index_xr.js file, beneath the declaration of the global variables, we called two new functions: init() and animate(). In Part 3 of this chapter's exercise, we will reconfigure the render call from our original main() function into two different functions: animate() and draw().

1. Beneath the closing curly brace of the init() function in index_xr.js, declare a function called animate with the following body:

```
function animate() {
    gl.setAnimationLoop(render);
}
```

Recall that the variable gl refers to the WebGL Renderer Three.js object we declared in the script's global scope and initialized in the function init(). Declaring the variable in the global scope allows us to access it in a function from outside the scope of the init() function's opening and closing curly braces. The method setAnimationLoop() on the Three.js WebGL Renderer object is a method provided by Three.js that replaces the call to requestAnimationFrame() in WebXR applications.

However, as was the case with the function requestAnimationFrame(), setAnimationLoop() accepts a callback function as its parameter. The method setAnimationLoop() will execute the value of its callback parameter once every frame.

For the callback function to be called by setAnimationLoop(), we can repurpose the render() function we wrote in Exercise 4.

2.   Repurpose the render function from the previous exercise as the callback function to be called by setAnimationLoop.

```
function render(time) {
    time *= 0.001;

    if (resizeDisplay) {
        camera.aspect = window.innerWidth / window.
        innerHeight;
        camera.updateProjectionMatrix();
    }

    cube.rotation.x += 0.01;
    cube.rotation.y += 0.01;
    cube.rotation.z += 0.01;

    sphere.rotation.x += 0.01;
    sphere.rotation.y += 0.01;
    sphere.rotation.y += 0.01;

    light.position.x = 20*Math.cos(time);
    light.position.y = 20*Math.sin(time);
    gl.render(scene, camera);
}
```

3. Finally, we can also repurpose the resizeDisplay()
    function from Exercise 4, and place it immediately
    beneath the closing brace of the render() function.

```
// UPDATE RESIZE
function resizeDisplay() {
    const canvas = gl.domElement;
    const width = canvas.clientWidth;
    const height = canvas.clientHeight;
    const needResize = canvas.width != width || canvas.
    height != height;
    if (needResize) {
        gl.setSize(width, height, false);
    }
    return needResize;
}
```

Save the index.html, index_xr.js, and VRButton.js files in your IDE and
launch your local development server. Navigate to the index.html page you
created for this exercise. If your browser supports WebXR, you should see the
Enter VR button we scripted. Pressing the button will launch the XR session
in your browser, displaying stereoscopic images inside your canvas. In the
final section of this chapter we will forward our site to a VR device connected
to our machine by USB and launch the Three.js scene in VR.

Enable Port Forwarding from a Local Development Server to a VR Device

The answer to the question of how to access a Web page from a connected
VR device running on a server on our local computer lies behind a flag
of the Microsoft Edge browser. As Edge and Google Chrome both use the
same JavaScript engine, the procedure to connect a USB-enabled device

with the output of a localhost is the same. For the steps to follow for other Web browsers, refer to the developer's documentation. However, for Edge and Chrome, the steps are as follows:

1. Navigate to [browser_name]://inspect/#devices.

    a. Replace browser_name with either Edge or Chrome.

2. Activate the checkbox next to Discover USB Devices.

3. Click the button labeled Port Forwarding.

4. In the menu that appears, add the port actively serving the Three.js scene on your localhost server.

    a. For example, my version of live-server through VS Code by default serves my files on port 5500.

5. In the field labeled "IP address and port" type: localhost:[your_port_number]

    a. Where [your_port_number] is the port on which your computer is serving the page containing the Three.js scene you'd like to load into a headset

6. Select Enable port forwarding and click done.

7. Do not close the page as it will sever port forwarding.

8. Open a command prompt in the folder where you saved the Android SDK/Platform-Tools folder.

9. Type adb devices.

10. Authorize the peripheral device to enable USB debugging.

To test whether port forwarding works between your browser and USB-connected device and, more importantly, if the steps we've taken to connect our Three.js scene to the WebXR API have achieved their aim, navigate to the localhost address of your Three.js application in the browser on your USB-attached VR headset. After the Web page loads, you should be presented with a 2D version of the Three.js scene on the homepage and a button near the page's bottom if the isSessionSupported() promise returns true in the VRButton.js script. If the button appears with the text 'Enter XR', click the button to enter the Three.js scene through the VR headset.

If the experience works, then you may notice that the scene places you directly beneath the sphere and cube rotating in the scene. To change the spawning location of the headset in VR, amend the camera position settings in the init() function in index_xr.js. Congratulations, you just created a WebXR application!

Part 3 Recap

In Part 3 of this exercise you:

- Separated the rendering logic of our application into the animate() function

- Kicked off the animation loop with the Three.js function setAnimationLoop

- Called the render function as a callback to run once every frame

- Moved the resize function into the render loop

- Used browser developer tools to forward the port serving the localhost

- Launched an ADB server from the command prompt

- Opened a Three.js VR scene through WebXR in a VR headset and its browser

Summary

Three.js is a library built atop the WebGL API that dramatically simplifies the steps required to create a simple, functioning XR scene. However, despite the strengths of Three.js, it cannot broadcast immersive scenes to peripheral XR devices alone. Fortunately, the Immersive Web Working Group has developed the functionality of the WebXR API to a point where we, as XR developers, can conveniently plug the rendering engine of our Three.js scenes into the event loop of an XR session in the browser. Together, Three.js and the WebXR API, by extending the already considerable power of the WebGL interface built into most modern browsers, provide a robust and accessible portal into the creation of mobile, immersive content.

In this chapter you:

- Set up USB debugging between a PC and Oculus Quest through Android Studio

- Downloaded and installed USB drivers to launch and run an ADB session in the command prompt

- Used the JavaScript Module design pattern to both export and import an HTML button element that contained logic to access the WebXR API

- Accessed the Navigator API of the browser to access the WebXR API

- Followed the steps suggested for the life cycle of a VR app defined by the Immersive Web Working group to create a program that safely launched an XR session in a secure browsing context

- Leveraged the principles of scope and closure in JS to launch an XR session from a script outside the application's main JS file

- Used the singleton design pattern to instantiate a single instance of a button class that accepted as a parameter the WebGL Rendering object of a Three.js scene

- Learned the meaning of a Promise object in JavaScript and used it to handle the request and response cycle of an XR session

- Used the DOM API's event handlers to provide the user with control to start and end an XR session

CHAPTER 7

Creating an Augmented Reality Website with Three.js and the WebXR API

We concluded the previous exercise by launching a virtual reality scene in an Oculus Quest through the browser. While the exercise accomplished its modest aims—to broadcast a Three.js scene from the browser to an XR device—it didn't offer much in terms of interactivity between a user and their scene. In this chapter we will begin to explore the role spatial tracking plays in the WebXR API. By providing convenient abstractions for complex matrix multiplication, the WebXR API and its affiliated spatial-tracking modules allow XR developers to create immersive experiences that make the most of the mobility so integral to the essence of the Web.

In this chapter you will:

- Download Node.JS and install Three.js through NPM, the Node package manager

- Use the `SessionInit` dictionary object in the WebXR API to request an augmented reality (AR) WebXR session

© Rakesh Baruah 2021
R. Baruah, *AR and VR Using the WebXR API*,
https://doi.org/10.1007/978-1-4842-6318-1_7

- Connect a Three.js WebGLRendering Context to an XR session

- Learn the role of reference spaces in the WebXR Spatial Tracking module

- Use the WebXR Hit Test module to place 3D objects in an AR scene

- Use WebXR Spatial Anchors to retain location data for 3D objects in AR

Exercise 6, Part 1: The Floating Cube

In Part 1 of this exercise we will review the process of creating a WebXR session in a Three.js application through the WebXR API. However, as this chapter focuses on AR, the following exercise will emphasize the "how" of creating a sense of immersion in 3D. The steps in this exercise will include:

1. Installing Three.js through the NPM

2. Outlining the application life cycle in a single JS file without the use of closure

3. Loading the Three.js scene components

4. Writing a function to initialize the application

5. Creating an HTML button to launch an XR session

6. Starting an AR session

7. Updating the state of the HTML button upon an AR session's launch

8. Saving a reference to the XR session

9. Connecting the XR session's rendering layer to the Three.js WebGLRendering context

10. Requesting a reference space from the WebXR API

11. Connecting the XR session to the Three.js scene

12. Writing a function to launch the Three.js animation loop

13. Replacing the HTML button's event handler to end an XR session

14. Resetting the state of the XR application

The source code for this book is available on GitHub via the book's product page, located at www.apress.com/gb/book/9781484263174.

Spatial Tracking in WebXR

Unlike virtual reality, scenes in AR must map a digital world onto an existing one. In AR scenes, spatial tracking becomes paramount. The spatial-tracking module of the WebXR API helps developers monitor the relative positions of objects, viewers, and environment in a scene. To maintain continuity through movement, AR scenes demand the calculation of a 3D object's position in its local coordinate space relative to the coordinate spaces of both the user and its environment. Using reference spaces, as defined by the WebXR API and its spatial-tracking module, we, as XR developers, can closely track and update the transformation matrices of different objects in a Three.js scene. The goal of Part 1 of this exercise is to help you understand the meaning of reference spaces in the WebXR API syntax and how their manipulation allows for the creation of immersive scenes augmented by 3D data.

In Part 1 of this exercise you will:

- Install three.js in an application through NPM

- Outline the life cycle of a WebXR application in a single JS file instead of using closure

219

- Create an HTML button to launch an AR session

- Use the `sessioninit` dictionary to request AR features for an XR session

- Launch an AR session asynchronously through an event handler

- Attach and remove event listeners from an AR session

- Use the WebXR function `updateRenderState()` to connect an XR session with a WebGL context

- Use 'reference spaces' to coordinate behavior between real life and an augmented environment

Install Three.js Through Node and the Node Package Manager

Create Files

Create an HTML document with a <script> tag pointing to an index.js file of `type=module`. Create the index.js file, too.

Download Node.js

Download Node.JS `https://nodejs.org/en/`.

Node.js is a JavaScript runtime that allows developers to write server-side code in JavaScript. Prior to the advent of Node.js, developers wrote server-side programs in languages other than JavaScript, like PHP, Perl, Java, and others. At one point, JavaScript was exclusively within the domain of front-end, or client-side, code. Recall, JavaScript began as a scripting language intended to facilitate the update of dynamic page elements. However, as the use and power of JavaScript expanded, some developers believed it was only rational that JS would provide the code for the Web's back end too. Though in this book we will not concern ourselves with server-side code, installing Node.js on our machines is a good exercise to go through, especially since JavaScript's popularity as a server-side language continues to rise. However, the real advantage for us in installing Node is the access it provides to the NPM: `www.npmjs.com/get-npm`.

Install Three.js Through NPM

NPM is like a giant library, in the literal sense. Conceptually, it stores packages, called modules, of code that each contain specific functionality to provide to an application. For example, if you'd like to quickly set up a Web server, you can download the HTTP module from NPM. There are thousands of packages available on NPM, each made by members of the Node community and available for free. One such module available for convenient download through NPM is Three.js.[1]

To install Three.js on our machines through NPM, we need only open the terminal in an IDE, like Visual Studio Code.

1. In VS code, navigate to the Terminal tab in the top menu bar and select New Terminal (Ctrl + Shift + `).

2. Navigate to the root of the folder in which you've created your HTML and JS pages.

3. Confirm you have Node properly installed by entering `node -v`.

   a. If you have Node properly installed, then you will see something like v12.18.0, the number of the Node version you installed.

4. Install Three.js by typing `npm i three`.

---

[1]Three.js "Readme" on NPM: `www.npmjs.com/package/three`

5. After NPM installs the Three.js library, you will see a folder called `node_modules/three` in the directory where you accessed NPM.

6. Import Three.js as a module into index.js.

    a. We import the Three.js Node module the same way we imported Three.js as an ES Module in previous exercises:

    ```
    import * as THREE from "../node_modules/three/
    build/three.module.js";
    ```

With Three.js installed on our machines and available in our application, we can begin to compose the functionality of our page.

Outline the Life Cycle of the Application

In this exercise we will write the functionality for the WebXR request and session life cycle without the use of closure. By encapsulating the functionality of the WebXR request and session life cycle in a single JavaScript file, we will be better able to focus on the details of creating and maintaining a WebXR session. Otherwise, the mechanics of scope and closure, while important to the execution of design patterns in JavaScript, may obfuscate the essential behavior of the WebXR API in a Three.js script. Here is an outline of the functions we will write in this exercise:

```
function loadScene() {
// setup the WebGL context and the components of a Three.js scene
}

function init() {
// kickoff the execution of the script
}
```

```
function onRequestSession() {
// handle the XR session request
}

function onSessionStarted() {
// handle the XR session once it has been created
}

function setupWebGLLayer() {
// connect the WebGL context to the XR session
}

function animate() {
// begin the animation loop
}

function render(time) {
// issue the draw command to the GPU
}

function endXRSession() {
// terminate the XR session
}

function onSessionEnd() {
// handle the 'end' event of the XR session
}
```

Now, let's define some global variables that we are going to need above our first function definition, loadScene():

```
// global scene values
var btn, gl, glCanvas, camera, scene, renderer, cube;

// global xr value
var xrSession = null;
```

Load the Scene Components

WebGL Context

As we have done several times by now, we will create a canvas element and WebGL context for our HTML page.

```
function loadScene() {
    // setup WebGL
    glCanvas = document.createElement('canvas');
    gl = glCanvas.getContext('webgl', { antialias: true });
    ...
}
```

Beneath the initialization of the gl variable, we will begin defining the objects required by a Three.js scene.

Perspective Camera

Recall from previous exercises that the constructor of a perspective camera in Three.js takes a field of view, aspect ratio, near clipping plane, and far clipping plane value as arguments.

```
    // setup Three.js scene
    camera = new THREE.PerspectiveCamera(
        70,
        window.innerWidth / window.innerHeight,
        0.01,
        1000
    );

    scene = new THREE.Scene();
```

You may experiment with the values of any of the perspective camera's variables. However, the WebXR API suggests near and far clipping plane values of 0.01, and 1000, or infinity, respectively.

Geometry, Material, and Mesh

Since our scene will feature a floating cube, let's proceed by creating geometry and material objects for the Three.js Mesh constructor.

```
var geometry = new THREE.BoxBufferGeometry(0.2, 0.2, 0.2);
var material = new THREE.MeshPhongMaterial({color: 0x89CFF0});
cube = new THREE.Mesh( geometry, material );
scene.add( cube );
```

While you may also use the Three.js BoxGeometry() constructor, it is best practice to create primitives from buffer geometry in Three.js, as they impact the performance of the scene less noticeably.

As we did in an earlier exercise, we'll use the MeshPhongMaterial in this scene. I've chosen the hexadecimal value for the color "baby blue." Take note that setting the color of a material object in Three.js requires the use of a JS object with a color attribute.

Hemisphere Light

You may also remember from an earlier exercise that a MeshPhongMaterial provides a specular shine to an object, which means the Phong material requires the presence of a light object in the scene. We've already used the directional light offered by Three.js, but let's use the Hemisphere Light object it offers, which takes as parameters to its constructor the color of the light, the color of the ground, and the light's intensity.

```
var light = new THREE.HemisphereLight( 0xffffff, 0xbbbbff, 1 );
            light.position.set( 0.5, 1, 0.25 );
            scene.add( light );
```

225

WebGLRenderer

Finally, to our `loadScene()` function we will add the code to set up our Three.js `WebGLRenderer`.

```
renderer = new THREE.WebGLRenderer({
    canvas: glCanvas,
    context: gl
});
renderer.setPixelRatio( window.devicePixelRatio );
renderer.setSize( window.innerWidth, window.innerHeight );
renderer.xr.enabled = true;
document.body.appendChild( renderer.domElement );
```

The most important features of the Three.js `WebGLRenderer` object are its canvas and context properties, and the activation of its `WebXR Manager` property. The reason why will become clear shortly.

Write the Body of the Initialize Function

Now that our `loadScene()` function is complete, we can turn our attention to the `init()` function we outlined. In the `init()` function, we will follow the steps suggested by the WebXR API for querying a user's capabilities to host a WebXR session.

Request the XR Session Mode

The mode of the WebXR session we'd like to test for is defined by the WebXR API as "immersive-ar."

```
function init() {
        navigator.xr.isSessionSupported('immersive-ar')
            .then((supported) => {
                if (supported) {
```

```
            // create button element to advertise XR
              btn = document.createElement("button");
           // add 'click' event listener to button
              btn.addEventListener('click', onRequestSession);
              btn.innerHTML = "Enter XR";
              var header = document.querySelector("header");
              header.appendChild(btn);
            }
            else {
            // create fallback session
                navigator.xr.isSessionSupported('inline')
                    .then((supported) => {
                        if (supported) {
                            console.log('inline session
                            supported');
                        }
                        else {console.log('inline not
                        supported')};
                    })
                }
            })
            .catch((reason) => {
                console.log('WebXR not supported: ' + reason);
            })
        }
```

Create Button Element to Advertise XR

If the user's browser and device support the queried XR mode, then the asynchronous function isSessionSupported('immersive-ar') will return a promise burrito that holds a true Boolean value. If the supported Boolean is true, then we will add a button to our home page. I included a

<header> element in the <body> of my home page, to which I've appended the button. You can do the same, if you'd like, by adding the following HTML code to the <body> tag of index.html:

```
<body>
    <header>
        <h1>Immersive AR with Three.js</h1>
    </header>
    <script type="module" src="index.js"></script>
</body>
```

If the supported promise burrito returns to us with a false Boolean value wrapped inside, then our program will enter the else block of our code.

Create 'inline' Fallback Option

The WebXR API suggests we provide our applications with the ability to fall back to simpler states if a user does not support the advanced features we request, like an "immersive-ar" mode. The mode 'inline' is one the WebXR API defines as a session that occurs in the HTML canvas of the page.

Write the Body of the Button's Event Listener

The function init() creates a button on the HTML page if a user's context supports an 'immersive-ar' mode. As the WebXR API requires that we ask the user before accessing the tracking information of their device, we present the button with an onclick handler that activates the XR session.

onRequestSession()

In the code we've written, we defined the listener for the click event as the function onRequestSession(). Let's define that function now.

228

```
function onRequestSession(){
    console.log("requesting session");
    navigator.xr.requestSession(
  'immersive-ar',
  {requiredFeatures: ['viewer', 'local']})
        .then(onSessionStarted)
        .catch((reason) => {
            console.log('request disabled: ' + reason.log);
        });
}
```

Again, we follow the WebXR API's instructions for requesting an XR session. The asynchronous requestSession() function on the browser's XR interface requires the mode of the session we'd like to request, as well as a SessionInit dictionary that contains any required or optional features.

The SessionInit Dictionary

The required features we've defined in the SessionInit dictionary are "reference spaces" as defined by the WebXR Spatial Tracking module. The WebXR API Spatial Tracking module defines several types of reference spaces: viewer, local, local-floor, bounded-floor, and unbounded.

Reference Spaces

First, we'll quickly review the reference spaces we will *not* use in this exercise. A bounded-floor reference space applies to an XR experience that asks the user to move around their physical environment without crossing the parameters of a fixed boundary as defined by the XR hardware. An unbounded reference space, on the other hand, allows a user to move freely and travel significant distances.

In this exercise, we will concern ourselves with `local` and `viewer` reference spaces, as defined by the WebXR API Spatial Tracking module. A `local` reference space allows for two types of experiences: one centered at the user's eye level and one centered at the user's floor. The `local-floor` reference space, which orients its world axis with its origin at the user's feet, is not available on all devices, though you may query for it as an optional feature in the `SessionInit` dictionary. The `local` reference space will initialize x, y, z, and orientation values near the viewer's position at the time of the session's creation, as conveyed by the XR device.

The `viewer reference` space, on the other hand, will always track with the user's XR device. Not only does the `viewer reference` space support `inline` experiences, ones in which the user's spatial tracking information is not relevant, but also experiences that leverage the WebXR API's Hit Test module, which we will address later in this chapter.

Start the AR Session

Once our application knows if the user's device supports the requested session and reference spaces we've requested, then we begin the XR session by accepting the promise burrito returned by the XR interface's `requestSession()` function.

onSessionStarted(session)

If the promise resolves to true, we add the function `onSessionStarted()` to the promise chain.

```
function onSessionStarted(session){
    console.log('starting session');

    ...
}
```

Once the XR session starts on the user's device, we have to alter the appearance of the button element that advertises the page's XR content.

Change the Button Element's State

Still within the onSessionStarted() function, we remove the listener on the button element that activates the XR session because the session has already begun; the WebXR API cannot run more than one XR session at a time. Requesting a second session while another runs will throw an error in the application.

Add/Remove Event Listeners

```
    ...
btn.removeEventListener('click', onRequestSession);
btn.addEventListener('click', endXRSession);
    ...
```

While removing one event listener, we add another; this one also listens for the button's click. However, unlike the event listener it is replacing, the new listener on the button element calls a function called endXRSession().

Update the Button's Text

Because our button element displays text advertising the beginning of an XR session upon the page's startup, we must change its appearance once an XR session has already begun.

```
    ...
btn.innerHTML = "STOP AR";
    ...
```

Save a Reference to the XR Session

Recall that we defined the xrSession variable as a global variable in the "Outline the Life Cycle of the Application" section of this exercise. Saving a reference to the XR session provides us with the ability to continuously access the attributes of the running session throughout the life cycle of our application.

```
xrSession = session;
```

Set the XR Session's XR WebGL Layer Property to Three.js Rendering Context

Still within the onSessionStarted() function, we take an opportunity to perform one of three critical tasks.

Critical Task #1: makeXRCompatible()

First, we set the area of the page to which we want the XR session to render our scene as the same area to which our Three.js scene will render its content. As an AR session merges the view of a device's camera with the view of an artificially rendered scene, it is important that the two image sources find a single target. We can accomplish this by calling and creating our own asynchronous function.

```
xrSession = session;
setupWebGLLayer()
    .then(()=> {
       // to be completed in Critical Task #2
    })
}
```

We call the function `setupWebGLLayer()` from within the `onSessionStarted()` function. We define it, however, in its own function declaration.

```
function setupWebGLLayer() {
    return gl.makeXRCompatible().then(() => {
        xrSession.updateRenderState(
{baseLayer: new XRWebGLLayer(xrSession, gl)});
    });
}
```

From inside the `setupWebGLLayer()` function, we continue with the execution of our first of three critical tasks during the launch of an XR session in concert with a Three.js scene. The WebGL context we saved in the variable `gl` includes within it, courtesy of the browser's APIs, an asynchronous function called `makeXRCompatible()`. Upon the receipt of the resolved promise burrito from the call to `gl.makeXRCompatible()`, we call a function made available to us through the WebXR API on the XR `session` object. That function is called `updateRenderState()`, which takes as an argument a dictionary object that sets the value of an XR session's `baseLayer` to a new `XRWebGLLayer`. An `XRWebGLLayer` is also an object provided to us through the WebXR API. It allows us to complete our first critical task; it connects the XR session with the WebGL context we defined as the context attribute on our Three.js WebGL Renderer in the `loadScene()` function.

With the promises on the `setupWebGLLayer()` asynchronous function fulfilled, our application's flow returns to the `onSessionStarted()` function where it entered the `setupWebGLLayer()` promise chain. For this convenience, we can thank the return keyword in the `setupWebGLLayer()` function. Upon fulfillment of `setupWebGLLayer()`'s promise, we call the next two critical functions of our XR session launch.

Set the XR Session's Reference Space for AR

The second critical function is the assignment of our Three.js WebXR Manager object's reference space.

Critical Task #2: setReferenceSpaceType(…):

Because our AR application will allow a user to walk within a limited area around the origin of the Three.js scene's launch, we know our experience requires at least a `local` reference space. That is, after all, what we requested on the session as a required feature in our `SessionInit` dictionary in the `onRequestSession()` function. In order for our Three.js scene to synchronize with the XR session we've requested from the WebXR API, we must set the reference space on the XR Manager of our Three.js scene to a `local` reference space too. Following the asynchronous call to the function `setupWebGLLayer()` from within the `onSessionStarted()` function, continue writing the promise chain.

```
setupWebGLLayer()
    .then(()=> {
    // continued from Critical Task #1
        renderer.xr.setReferenceSpaceType('local');
        ...
```

Three.js offers us access to the `XR Manager` it automatically creates for us upon the construction of an XR enabled `WebGLRenderer` through the renderer's `xr` property. By calling the Three.js function `setReferenceSpaceType('local')` on our renderer's `xr` property, we can set the reference space of our Three.js scene to match the reference space of our XR session. By ensuring that the reference space between the XR session and the Three.js renderer match, we will better prepare a user's device to render the content of our scene as we have planned.

Set the Three.js XR Manager's XR Session Property to the Current XR Session

Here, we execute the third critical step of our application: we set the XR session requested through the WebXR API to the session whose frames the Three.js renderer will paint to our scene.

Critical Task #3: setSession(xrSession)

Immediately below renderer.xr.setReferenceSpaceType('local') write:

```
renderer.xr.setSession(xrSession);
```

Even though a call to the WebXR API for an 'immersive-ar' session informs our device to display its camera view as our app's background, our Three.js scene has no intrinsic idea of this decision. If left uninformed, the Three.js renderer will continue to paint the scene to the HTML canvas, which the user's device won't even show if in an AR mode. However, by connecting the XR session with the Three.js renderer, the animation loop called from within Three.js will render to the same WebGL context as the device's camera.

With the three critical functions of our XR session launch executed, we close the onSessionStarted() function with a call to a function we have created and named animate().

Call the animate( ) Function

Here, for reference, is the onSessionStarted(session) function in its entirety:

```
function onSessionStarted(session){
    console.log('starting session');
    btn.removeEventListener('click', onRequestSession);
    btn.addEventListener('click', endXRSession);
```

```
    btn.innerHTML = "STOP AR";
    xrSession = session;
    setupWebGLLayer()
        .then(()=> {
            renderer.xr.setReferenceSpaceType('local');
            renderer.xr.setSession(xrSession);
            animate();
        })
}
```

Appropriately, the onSessionStarted() function completes by calling the function animate(), which kicks off our scene's animation loop.

Call Three.js' SetAnimationLoop() with the render() Function Set as Its Callback

To start the animation loop for our scene, we fit the body of the animate() function with a call to the built-in function provided by Three.js, setAnimationLoop().

```
function animate() {
    renderer.setAnimationLoop(render);
}
```

Define the Body of the render() Function

By providing the render function to the function setAnimationLoop() as an argument, we instruct Three.js to call our render function once every frame.

```
function render(time) {
    renderer.render(scene, camera);
}
```

In turn, the render function executes the rendering of the Three.js scene.

Create an Event Handling Function for the End of a Session

Recall that in the "Change the Button Element's State" section of this exercise, we replaced the click event listener on the button element from onRequestSession to endXRSession. Here, let's define the body of the callback function activated by the user clicking the button on our HTML page if an XR session is current.

```
function endXRSession() {
    if (xrSession) {
        console.log('ending session...');
        xrSession.end().then(onSessionEnd);
    }
}
```

The end() function is one provided to us through the WebXR API as a method on the XR session object. As it is an asynchronous function, we can call another function upon the fulfillment of its promise.

Create a Function to Reset the State of the Application

In this final function, we reset the state of our xrSession global variable to null; we reset the text of the html button that launches the XR session request; and we remove the click event listener we just called and replace it with the listener that will relaunch an XR request.

```
function onSessionEnd() {
    xrSession = null;
    console.log('session ended');
    btn.innerHTML = "START AR";
    btn.removeEventListener('click', endXRSession);
    btn.addEventListener('click', onRequestSession);
}
```

Saving the HTML and JS file, launching the local Web server, and forwarding the page to a connected AR-capable device through ADB and Chrome's dev tools will show the cube hovering in your space. Depending on the processing speed of your connected device, it may take a moment for the tracking capabilities of the WebXR API to kick in. Once they do, however, walk around the cube in your scene. Notice that it remains at its instantiated origin relative to the movement of your device. As the cube has as its coordinate plane the dimensions defined by the `local` reference space, and your device has as its coordinates the `viewer` reference space, the two move relative to each other. That is the underlying power and beauty of the WebXR API's Spatial Tracking tools. The reference spaces provided by the WebXR API define the relationships between two or more coordinate planes, thus allowing for AR experiences that create the illusion of an immersive reality.

To make the scene come more alive, try to use what we have covered in this exercise and in previous ones to add rotation and a slight bobbing motion to the cube. To see an example of the code to execute these features, visit the exercise's source code, available on the book's product page at `www.apress.com/9781484263174`.

Part 1 Recap

- Installed Three.js in an application through NPM

- Outlined the life cycle of a WebXR application in a single JS file without using closure

- Created an HTML button to launch an AR session

- Used the `sessionInit` dictionary to request AR features for an XR session

- Launched an AR session asynchronously through an event handler

- Attached and removed event listeners from an AR session

- Used the WebXR function `updateRenderState()` to connect an XR session with a WebGL context

- Used 'reference spaces' to coordinate behavior between real life and an augmented environment

Exercise 6, Part 2: The Hit Test

The purpose of Part 1 of this exercise was to illustrate how the WebXR API's Spatial Tracking module simplified creating immersive scenes by handling the computation required to resolve two relative coordinate spaces. In Part 2 of the exercise we will again use the Spatial Tracking module, but this time in concert with the Hit Test module, also provided by the WebXR API.

The WebXR Hit Test module encapsulates the computer vision algorithms used to calculate distance between a device and an object, virtual or real. Using the premise of a ray cast, the Hit Test module sends a ray from a source, such as a phone, and calculates the distance between the source and an object the ray intersects. The Hit Test module contains logic that not only determines intersection with a real-world plane but also locates the position of the intersection in local coordinate space. The functions in the Hit Test and Spatial Tracking modules make it possible for us to create an AR application that places 3D shapes at locations we tap through the screens on our phones.

In this exercise you will:

- Manipulate a phone as a controller through the WebXR Device API

- Create a reticle object to track a user's ray cast

- Reimplement closure to keep a Hit Test running

- Use the WebXR Hit Test module to request a Hit Test source

- Use the WebXR Spatial Anchors module to retain the location data of 3D objects added to a real environment

Controllers and Events

To begin this part of the exercise, let's address some simple housekeeping in our project folders.

Set Up Files and Variables

Copy the index.html and index.js files from Part 1. Save them in a new folder within the project's root. Keeping the files in the same root folder as the files from Part 1 means we do not have to install a duplicate folder containing the NPM files we installed locally. Also, replace the global variables in the new index.js page, which I have renamed hit_test.js.

```
// global scene values
var btn, gl, glCanvas, camera, scene, renderer;
var controller, reticle;

// global xr value
var xrSession = null;
var xrViewerPose;
var hitTestSource = null;
var hitTestSourceRequested = false;
```

In the "Geometry, Material, and Mesh" section of Part 1, we created the cube we rotated in our scene. In this step, we will replace that code with code that creates a controller, a geometry buffer, and an event handler.

Get a Controller

After removing the code from Part 1 that created the cube and added it to our scene, replace it with code to call the Three.js method to access a device's controllers.

```
controller = renderer.xr.getController(0);
controller.addEventListener('select', onSelect);
scene.add(controller);
```

If you're anything like me, then you may be wondering what in the world a controller variable could be referring to on a device such as a phone.

WebXR Device API

It turns out that Three.js offers the `getController()` method on its renderer's `XR Manager` property as an abstraction of the WebXR Device API. Under its hood, the WebXR Device API tracks, among other things, a ray cast from a user's device. The argument `0` in the Three.js `getController()` function maps to the creation of a target ray matching the XR frame from the perspective of the viewer's reference space.

Define Buffer Geometry

As our application will generate shapes at the coordinates where we tap our device's screen, we must write a function to efficiently create the shapes. First, we must define what kind of shapes we'd like to instantiate. Still in the `loadScene()` function, add the following:

```
var geometry = new THREE.CylinderBufferGeometry(0.1, 0.1, 0.2, 32)
  .translate(0, 0.1, 0);
```

241

As the function to generate the shapes fires on every controller 'select' event, we define a function to serve as a handler for the event. We define the buffer geometry before passing it into the Mesh constructor inside the onSelect callback function.

onSelect() Callback Function

Three.js offers another abstraction through its WebXRController library that handles any events dispatched through one of its controller objects. By defining a 'select' event on our Three.js controller object, Three.js knows that we would like to track an event dispatched from a controller. Inside the loadScene() function, define a new function.

```
function onSelect() {
console.log("on select fired...");
    // generate a random color for the geometry
var material = new THREE.MeshPhongMaterial(
{ color: 0xffffff * Math.random() } );
    // create the mesh for the geometry and its material
    var mesh = new THREE.Mesh(geometry, material);
    // position the geometry at the position of the reticle
    mesh.applyMatrix4(reticle.matrix); // THIS IS A KEY FUNCTION
    // randomly set the geometry's scale
    mesh.scale.y = Math.random() * 2 + 1;
    scene.add(mesh);
}
```

As no other input sources exist for an experience running exclusively on a phone in AR (yet), Three.js defaults to a screen tap as the event for which a controller listens.

We'll come back to the function that applies a new matrix to the cylinder's mesh in the "reticle.matrix.fromArray(...)" section near the end of this exercise.

Create the Reticle

Before we can apply the matrix of the reticle to the cylinder mesh created by the onSelect() event, we must of course define what the heck a reticle is. In the loadScene() function, beneath the declaration of the controller object, define the value of the reticle object.

```
reticle =    new THREE.Mesh(
new THREE.RingBufferGeometry(0.15, 0.2, 32).rotateX(-Math.PI / 2),
    new THREE.MeshBasicMaterial({color: "#00FF00"})
    );
```

A reticle is a conventional term used to describe a visual marker for hit testing. The shape of the reticle we will use will be a green ring rotated 90 degrees to be parallel with the ground.

Set the Reticle Object's Properties

As the reticle will mark the point of intersection between the ground plane and the ray cast from a user's phone, it should *not* update its own transform, or position matrix.

```
        reticle.matrixAutoUpdate = false;
        reticle.visible = false;
        scene.add(reticle);
```

The reticle's position in the scene will be determined by the intersection of a viewer's ray cast and a plane detected in the camera feed. That is, after all, the point of our hit test.

Move XR Query Function

Unlike Part 1 of this exercise, we will check if an XR session of mode 'immersive-ar' is supported by a user's device in the *same* function that loads our scene, loadScene().

```
navigator.xr.isSessionSupported('immersive-ar')
      .then((supported) => {
        if (supported) {
              btn = document.createElement("button");
              btn.addEventListener('click',
              onRequestSession);
              btn.innerHTML = "Enter XR";
              var header = document.
              querySelector("header");
              header.appendChild(btn);
        }
          else {
              navigator.xr.isSessionSupported('inline')
              .then((supported) => {
                    if (supported) {
                    console.log('inline session
                    supported')
                    }
                    else {console.log('inline not
                    supported')};
              })
          }
      })
      .catch((reason) => {
              console.log('WebXR not supported: ' +
              reason);
      });
```

The reason why we must make the change to the code in Part 2 has everything to do with our old friend, closure.

The Return of Closure

By creating the button element in the same function housing the onSelect() event handler in its scope, we are able to make sure that our controllers and geometry buffers remain alive when our hit tests occur. Now, we update the HTML button's 'click' event listener.

onRequestSession()

In Part 2 of this exercise, the value of the WebXR API's sessionInit dictionary becomes more apparent. In the "onRequestSession()" section of Part 1, we requested an XR session with an 'immersive-ar' mode and required features of both 'viewer' and 'local' reference spaces. However, in an XR session that implements the Hit Test module, those features are *assumed*. The value of the "required features'" key in the sessionInit dictionary for a Hit Test application is, appropriately, a 'hit-test', which we enter between brackets per the API's specification.

Beneath the closing bracket of the loadScene() function in hit_test.js, define the onRequestSession() function.

```
function onRequestSession() {
    console.log("requesting session");
    navigator.xr.requestSession('immersive-ar',
    {requiredFeatures: ['hit-test'], optionalFeatures:
    ['local-floor']})
        .then(onSessionStarted)
        .catch((reason) => {
            console.log('request disabled: ' + reason);
        });
}
```

In addition to "required features," the WebXR `sessionInit` dictionary accepts a key defined as "optional features." The 'local-floor' parameter is a feature that facilitates with a Hit Test. Because all devices are not equipped with the technology to implement the 'local-floor' feature, we set its flag to optional.

onSessionStarted(...)

The `onSessionStarted()` function for Part 2 remains unchanged from Part 1. You can place it beneath the closing brace of the `onRequestSession()` function.

```
function onSessionStarted(session) {
    console.log('starting session');
    btn.removeEventListener('click', onRequestSession);
    btn.addEventListener('click', endXRSession);
    btn.innerHTML = "STOP AR";
    xrSession = session;
    setupWebGLLayer()
        .then(()=> {
            renderer.xr.setReferenceSpaceType('local');
            renderer.xr.setSession(xrSession);
            animate();
        })
}
```

The only function remaining from Part 1 that we must adapt for Part 2 is the render function, which handles the logic of the application's hit tests.

WebXR Spatial Anchors Module

The new code in the render function will implement the main functionality of the WebXR API Hit Test Module. The two core elements are the **requestHitTestSource()** and **getHitTestResults()** functions. Both are provided by the WebXR API, meaning we as developers have little to do but call the functions. However, it is helpful to understand why we are calling them.

requestHitTestSource()

The primary purpose of the algorithm wrapped in the requestHitTestSource() function is to capture the location information of a *viewer's device* at every moment a target ray intersects a plane in the real world. If the computer vision algorithm wrapped in the requestHitTestSource() function detects an intersection between a ray cast from the viewer's device and a plane in the environment, it saves the *position information of the user's device at that moment.* That is why both the time and the frame are essential to the operation of our revamped render function.

XR Frame and Time

Amend the render function to accept both time and the XR frame as arguments. Then compose the following conditionals inside the body of the function:

```
function render(time, frame) {
      if (frame) {
              var referenceSpace = renderer.
              xr.getReferenceSpace('local');
              var session = frame.session;
          // viewerPose provided by Spatial Tracking Module
              xrViewerPose = frame.getViewerPose(referenceSpace);
```

```
                if (hitTestSourceRequested === false) {
                        session.requestReferenceSpace
                        ("viewer").then((referenceSpace) => {
  session.requestHitTestSource({space: referenceSpace})
            .then((source) => {
                hitTestSource = source;})
});

                        session.addEventListener("end", () => {
                                hitTestSourceRequested = false;
                                hitTestSource = null;
                        });
                }

                if (hitTestSource) {
                        var hitTestResults = frame.getHitTestRe
                        sults(hitTestSource);

                        if (hitTestResults.length > 0) {
                                var hit = hitTestResults[0];
                                reticle.visible = true;
                                reticle.matrix.fromArray(hit.
                                getPose(referenceSpace).
                                transform.matrix);
                        } else {
                                reticle.visible = false;
                        }
                }
        }

        renderer.render(scene, camera);
}
```

With a hit test source position recognized and saved, we can write our render function to use the position information of a hit to draw our reticle to the user's screen.

getHitTestResults( )

The WebXR-provided function getHitTestResults() performs a calculation using the relationship between the viewer and local reference spaces we defined earlier in the program. At its core, the function calculates the distance *between* the viewer's device and the intersected plane. The algorithm then calculates the position of the intersection of the viewer's ray and the environment plane in *local* coordinates. In other words, the getHitTestResults() function has transformed the position of an intersection recorded from the perspective of the viewer into the objective, local coordinates of the world. By doing so, the function employs the spatial anchors features of the WebXR API's Spatial Anchors module, which saves the location information of each hit test result as a transform matrix.

reticle.matrix.fromArray(…)

Finally, we close our revised render function by setting the position and orientation values of the reticle through its transform matrix, which we populate from the 16 elements of the array defining the hit test result's position in local coordinates.

Running the Scene

Upon running the scene, you may find that it takes a few seconds for your device's position tracking to kick in. However, once the application recognizes the planes in your environment, it will begin tracking intersections with the reticle. Pressing the screen while the reticle is visible in the scene will generate a Three.js cylinder object at the point where the device's emitted ray intersects a plane in your environment. Notice that the reticle's orientation matches the orientation of the planes it intersects—it rotates 90 degrees for walls, for example. If your application behaves with satisfying results, then we can consider this Hit Test a success.

Part 2 Recap

- Saved a reference to a controller through the WebXR Device API

- Attached a 'select' listening event to the controller

- Instantiated geometry using Three.js geometry buffer object

- Used the get and set reference space functions from the WebXR Spatial Tracking module to save state of relative coordinate spaces

- Used the `requestHitTestSource()` function from the WebXR Hit Test module to capture the origin point of a ray cast sent from the user's device

- Used the `getHitTestResults()` function from the WebXR Hit Test module to create an array of spatial anchors in a scene

- Used the `getPose()` function from the WebXR Spatial Tracking module to capture the position of a ray's intersection with a plane in local coordinate space

- Used the `fromArray()` method on the reticle object to store the transform from a hit test into a 16 bit array

- Used the `mesh.applyMatrix4()` function to copy the position coordinates of the reticle to a cylinder object

- Instantiated a cylinder object with random color and scale in an AR scene

Summary

The WebXR API offers several modules through which it fine tunes the capabilities it offers developers. For example, in addition to its core API, the WebXR API provides extensions through its AR module, its Spatial Tracking module, its Spatial Anchors module, its Hit Test module, and its Device module. While the functionality of all the toys hidden inside the evolving WebXR API can overwhelm developers, WebGL abstractions like Three.js significantly lighten the load.

Three.js conveniently lies atop the WebXR API, offering interfaces to much of the API's most popular features without hiding them beneath unnecessary bloatware. As the World Wide Web continues to integrate itself with our daily lives, it's reasonable to assume that augmented and virtual features of the internet will ingratiate themselves, too. The WebXR API is still in its early infancy; its fire is only a flicker, but its future is undoubtedly bright.

In the next chapter we will move back into virtual reality, yet take with us the tools we have picked up regarding interaction in XR space. Using the A-Frame framework, an abstraction built on top of Three.js, we will create an immersive VR exercise that aims to leverage the full provisions of a device like the Oculus Quest.

In this chapter you:

- Installed Node.js and through its packet manager, NPM, downloaded Three.js as a module

- Used the WebXR API AR module to request and create an immersive-ar session

- Learned to set the required and optional features of a requested XR session through the `xrSessionInit` dictionary provided by the WebXR API

- Used the `setSession()` function in Three.js to sync the Three.js renderer's animation loop to the properties of the XR session

- Used the `makeXRCompatible()` function to ensure WebGL context compatibility with an XR session's `XRWebGLLayer`.

- Implemented the `requestHitTestSource()` and `getHitTestResult()` methods from the WebXR API's Hit Test module to calculate the position of intersections between rays cast from the viewer and planes in the real-world environment

- Leveraged the features of the WebXR API's Spatial Anchors module to save the position data of 3D objects generated dynamically in an augmented reality WebXR scene

CHAPTER 8

Building VR for the Web with A-Frame

In this chapter we will return to creating a virtual reality experience through the WebXR API. Though we used the Three.js library and the WebXR API to create a virtual reality scene in exercise 5, in this chapter we will use the A-Frame framework. However, before we jump into the creative process with A-Frame, let's review what we've learned so far in this course.

A Review So Far

We began this course with an introduction into the elements of WebGL, the API on which the WebXR API builds. By experimenting with the fundamentals of WebGL in the browser, we learned the following:

- 3D on the Web occurs on the HTML canvas element.

- The WebGL API uses the power of a GPU to render vertices and pixels.

- OpenGL ES is the specification of WebGL that defines the communication between a server and a client GPU.

- The WebGL API allows developers to write OpenGL Shading Language (GLSL) code with JavaScript.

© Rakesh Baruah 2021
R. Baruah, *AR and VR Using the WebXR API*,
https://doi.org/10.1007/978-1-4842-6318-1_8

- The Web browser includes many APIs like the WebGL and Canvas APIs.

- Another API the browser implements is the WebXR API.

- The WebXR API builds atop the WebGL API and extends features of other browser APIs like the Canvas API and the Gamepad API.

- As WebGL is an implementation for creating graphics and rendering them to a screen; it does not implement logic to facilitate convenient writing of Web programs.

Once familiar with the requirements and syntax of WebGL, we moved our attention to an abstraction of WebGL, the JavaScript library known as Three.js. In the chapters dedicated to Three.js, we learned:

- Developers created Three.js to abstract the low-level details of WebGL into a JavaScript library that allows Web programmers to more comfortably work with WebGL and OpenGL ES.

- While Three.js abstracts the functionality of WebGL into familiar JavaScript properties and functions, the WebXR API serves as a conduit between a Web application written in Three.js and the hardware elements of an XR device, such as a mobile phone or standalone VR headset.

- Through the WebXR API, developers can create Three.js programs that not only render 3D graphics to a screen but also interface with an assortment of XR devices.

You'd be forgiven for thinking that with knowledge of both WebGL and Three.js under our belts, we know everything there is to know about creating XR applications for the Web. While it is true that we can make full use of the WebXR API through only WebGL and Three.js, this course would not be complete without a lesson on perhaps the most convenient and simplified, though not simple, tool for creating WebXR applications. That tool is called A-Frame, and it is the subject of this chapter and its exercises.

What Is A-Frame?

Developed by Mozilla, the team behind Firefox, A-Frame is a framework for creating Three.js applications. A framework is to a Web application as an A-frame is to a house, for example. In engineering, an A-Frame is a simple structure made up of two beams positioned 45 degrees from the ground and attached at their adjoining ends, forming the outline of a letter "A". The A-frame, therefore, is a skeleton of a structure, the armature that supports the design.

Similarly, A-Frame, as a framework for Three.js, provides a set of rules and conveniences that place the writing of Three.js applications more closely in line with HTML documents. As has been the case with many other concepts in this course, perhaps it'll be best to reach an understanding of A-Frame as a framework for Three.js by creating a simple scene. For Part 1 of Exercise 7, let's build a basic scene in A-Frame that contains a sky, a light, a ground, a cube, and a material.

Exercise 7, Part 1: The Bare Bones of A-Frame

In Part 1 of this exercise you will:

- Learn how to create an A-Frame application

- Place 3D primitives in an A-Frame scene

Installation

There are two convenient ways to install the A-Frame framework in a Web application. One is through the <script> tag in the head of an HTML document, which we have already done many times before. The second way is through NPM, the Node Package Manager. As this is an introductory lesson into A-Frame, let's use the first method, with which we are well familiar.

From the Web

To install A-Frame, navigate to the A-Frame website (aframe.io) and copy the source data for an HTML script element, or copy it from the following code. The most recent version of A-Frame, as of this writing, is version 1.0.4. Refer to the official A-Frame documentation at aframe.io.docs for up-to-date status.

```
<head>
<script src="https://aframe.io/releases/1.0.4/aframe.min.js">
</script>
</head>
```

Place the A-Frame script tag in the <head> section of an HTML document in a code editor like Visual Studio Code. Save the document as index.html in a folder that you recognize.

And that's it!

Abstraction FTW!

As we've seen throughout this course, subsequent technologies in the WebXR ecosystem build upon their predecessors. WebGL, for example, built upon OpenGL ES; the WebXR API built upon the WebGL API; Three. js built upon WebGL; and now we see that A-Frame builds upon Three.js. The stacking of these technologies on top of each other, each abstracting a bit of its underlying source, results in an elegant, simple product like

A-Frame. If you recall the amount of code we had to write in Chapters 3 and 4 of this course to create a WebGL application, then, by simply installing A-Frame in a Web document, you've witnessed the power and beauty of abstraction.

Abstraction Takes Some L's

However, with a library or framework's abstraction of its influence, tools and practices with which we've become familiar crawl deeper into hiding. For some technical practices, like driving a sports car, relying on an abstraction like an automatic transmission relieves the operator of the stress introduced by too many variables. Yet, for other practices, like cooking, too much abstraction becomes an obstacle in itself. You may know how to cut a cucumber, for example; but can you dice one up using this fancy, new gadget I just bought online that's solar powered, connected to the Internet, and smart, and automated, and Bluetooth capable? Here, the instructions are in Japanese! Like other abstractions of complex technologies, A-Frame provides convenience through simplicity. Yet, it also asks for a new way of thinking.

The Entity Component System

In game design, and in any design practice for that matter, creational patterns have emerged through iteration by bright minds. In an earlier exercise we implemented one such pattern called the Singleton pattern,[1] which abstracted the behavior of a program through the interface of a single JavaScript object, the VR Button. Another design pattern, particularly popular for game design, is called the Entity Component System (ECS), and it is the premise on which A-Frame has been built.

---

[1]In software engineering, the singleton pattern is a software design pattern that restricts the instantiation of a class to one "single instance." This is useful when exactly one object is needed to coordinate actions across the system.

ECS vs. OOP

An ECS isn't that much different from a program created with another popular design paradigm called object-oriented programming, commonly referred to as OOP. In OOP, developers create classes that generalize the properties and behaviors of objects. A Soldier class, for example, may have as properties a name, an ID number, and a unit to which the soldier belongs. Behaviors, or methods, encapsulated within the Soldier class may include running, jumping, shooting, and crawling, for example. In a game where soldiers are characters, a platoon might consist of 12 soldiers, each an instance of the Soldier class, and each with unique values to common attributes. Every soldier has a name, ID, and specialty, for example, but they may not be the same. Each soldier inherits common traits from their parent class. While the OOP model has been and still is very popular in many programming domains, it has been replaced in some applications that require a tremendous number of moving parts, like game design.

Composition over Inheritance

A common frustration among game designers with the OOP paradigm is with what to many is one of OOP's greatest strengths: inheritance. One of the guiding principles of software development goes by the acronym DRY. Abbreviating "do not repeat yourself," DRY reminds programmers that code written once is best reused rather than rewritten. The convenience of inheritance in the OOP paradigm follows from the premise of DRY; classes can inherit common attributes and behaviors from parent classes, extending broad base classes to create more nuanced collections of objects. Where some developers, especially in game design, find fault in the tenet of inheritance is in its union with another set of problems created by tightly coupled code.

Tightly coupled code is a prelude, and often euphemism, for a far more egregious nightmare in the dream life of a game developer: spaghetti code. Tightly coupled code is like the string of Christmas, or decorative lights one hangs from bushes and trees, or walls in college dormitories. If wired in series, the entire string of lights will malfunction when a single bulb expires. To fix such a string of lights, one would have to check each individual bulb: a time consuming task for a set of three dozen light bulbs. Now, imagine the frustration you'd feel if instead of 36 bulbs, you'd have to check 36,000 lines of code for the one line of inoperability. No bueno!

In highly dependent but quickly performing applications, like mixed reality and gaming, for example, developers have eschewed complete reliance on the OOP paradigm for one that privileges composition over inheritance. A system that implements such a paradigm is called an Entity Component System, and beginning to understand the rationale behind its existence helps explain its use.

A-Frame: An Entity Component System-Based Framework for Three.js

The Three.js library had features of OOP. Meshes, for example, inherited from the Object3D base class; the WebXRManager extended the WebGLRenderer object. However, Three.js also offered glimpses of an entity component model. Geometries and materials, together, made up a mesh object; buffer objects had properties that defined a primitive's geometry; and textures included filters that operated as components that changed an image's appearance. As a framework for Three.js, A-Frame extends and expands the principle of composition already prevalent in the fabric of Three.js.

The Entity

A distinguishing characteristic of A-Frame is that it's written in declarative HTML syntax, like a traditional, 2D webpage. To add a scene object to an A-Frame application, all one must do is add a scene tag to the body of an HTML document.

```
<body>
    <a-scene>

    </a-scene>
</body>
```

And that's, literally, it. If you fire up your local host development server and visit the index.html page to which we've just added the A-Frame scene tag, you've just created an A-Frame application! That's all well and good, but what exactly did we just do?

Abstractions All the Way Down

Remember, A-Frame is an abstraction of Three.js, which is, in turn, an abstraction of WebGL. As an abstraction of an abstraction, A-Frame hides a lot of the plumbing, nuts, and bolts required to create an XR-enabled Web application. However, perusing A-Frame's documentation and source code, which is openly available on GitHub, we learn what A-Frame's scene element abstracts. What's the answer? Dang near everything!

Entities: Abstractions of Components

Contained within the scene entity in A-Frame is a collection of components, members of which may strike you as friendly, familiar chums. They are, among others: an active Three.js camera; a reference to a canvas element; a THREE.Scene object; and a THREE.WebGLRenderer in a component called, conveniently, "renderer". The scene tag in A-Frame

260

is an entity that includes components that make up the core state and behavior of a Three.js, WebXR application. With one tag in A-Frame we've instantiated no less than four Three.js objects, the creation of each would have required at least one line of JavaScript without A-Frame. Hopefully, you now see the elegance and simplicity of a framework abstraction like A-Frame.

The Component

So far we've seen the implementation of an entity in A-Frame, but what's all this talk about components? Components, in A-Frame, are objects that define the character of an entity. Components built into the A-Frame library include an animation component, a background component, a camera component, a 3D-model component, and a touch-control component, just to name a few.

Components Individualize Entities

If an entity became a scene through the application of a few components, such as a renderer, canvas, and camera, then how can we transform a generic entity into a 3D object like a plane?

```
<a-scene>
  <a-entity      geometry="primitive: plane; height: 10; width: 10"
rotation="-90 0 0"
material="side: double color: #fff">
  </a-entity>
</a-scene>
```

Viola! The components comprising the entity make the plane. The geometry component provides the buffer array for a primitive property we can define as a plane, box, circle, cone, or whatever other primitive shape A-Frame provides. The rotation component is a component inherent to all A-Frame entities, and the material component is one whose properties we can define with values to our liking. As A-Frame composes 3D scenes declaratively through HTML, we define A-Frame entities like HTML elements and A-Frame components like HTML attributes, setting the value of their properties through the use of the ":" character as with CSS styles.

Primitives

Of course, A-Frame wouldn't be all that convenient if every primitive shape we hoped to include in an XR scene we had to create from generic entities. Fortunately, the A-Frame library provides an assortment of commonly used primitive objects as premade, ready-to-use entities.

Add a Primitive Entity to a Scene Entity

One such primitive is the <a-box> entity. Let's add one to our scene:

```
<a-scene>
  ...
  <a-box color="tomato" depth="0.5" height="0.5" width="0.1"></a-box>
</a-scene>
```

As primitives in A-Frame are precomposed entities, we can forgo wrapping their components in generic `<entity>` tags. Each primitive in A-Frame comes with a collection of attributes we can choose to either define or leave to their default values. You can find the full collection of primitive shapes provided by A-Frame on the framework's website: `aframe.io`.

In addition to the more obvious attributes a primitive shape may have, like its color and dimensions, A-Frame primitives offer convenient access to more complex properties like image textures and materials. To add an image file to our scene as a material, we can make use of A-Frame's Asset Management System.

Systems

Whereas the E and the C in the ECS acronym stand for "entity" and "component," respectively, the S stands for "system." In A-Frame's ECS pattern, a system provides global scope, services, and management to classes of components. The Asset Manager is one type of system provided by A-Frame. The Asset Management System provides the core functionality of preloading assets, like images, an XR scene may require to run.

Add A-Frame's Asset Management System

We define the Asset Management System as an entity within an A-Frame scene. We define assets to be preloaded by the system as `<a-asset-item>` entities if they are miscellaneous assets such as 3D models and materials, or, more specifically, as `<img>`, `<audio>`, or `<video>` entities depending on the asset between the Asset Manager's tags.

```
<a-scene>
  <a-assets>
    <img id="brick" src="brick_mat.jpg"></img>
  </a-assets>
...
```

The Material Component

The material component in A-Frame comes with attributes like "`src`" and "`roughness`." We may set the value of multiple attributes built into an A-Frame component by separating each with a semicolon, as we do with CSS properties. To set the brick image I uploaded to my project folder on the `<a-box>` primitive in our scene, I can access the attributes of the material component inherently provided by the `<a-box>` primitive entity.

```
<a-box position="0.3 1.5 -0.5" material="src: #brick;
roughness: 1;" depth="0.5" height="0.5" width="0.5"></a-box>
<a-sky color="#87CEEB"></a-sky>
```

Set Component Properties Through Attributes

Like components, systems added to the syntax tree of an A-Frame page provide specific attributes. For example, notice in the previous step that I added a premade `<a-sky>` entity to the scene. I set the value of its color attribute to the RGB HEX value for a light blue. Loading an asset like an image into an A-Frame scene through the Asset Management System makes use of the system's feature of preloading files required by a scene.

Part 1 Recap

- Installed the A-Frame framework through an HTML script tag

- Abstracted the Three.js objects required for a WebXR scene by placing an A-Frame `<a-scene>` element within the markup of an HTML document

- Used the ECS pattern by defining a generic entity with the components of a 3D plane

- Leveraged the A-Frame library to place a precomposed `<a-box>` entity in the scene

- Implemented the built-in A-Frame Asset Management System to preload a texture to the `<a-box>` entity's material component

- Simply defined the color value of a `<a-sky>` element through the entity's color component

As with entities, A-Frame allows developers to custom-build components specific to their scenes. As A-Frame is simply a framework atop Three.js, we can use what we've already learned from our exercises with the Three.js library to construct A-Frame projects richer in detail and experience.

Using Three.js in A-Frame

Before we build a custom component in A-Frame, we should ask ourselves what A-Frame lacks that we'd like to add to our scene. One glaring problem with the scene we created in Part 1 of this exercise is the heavy artifacting that occurs on the brick material we applied to our <a-box> element. As you may recall from exercise 4 in Chapter 5, Three.js provides properties through its texture and material objects that allow us to fine-tune the settings applied to assets. First extending A-Frame through Three.js will set us on the road toward creating A-Frame components of our own.

Exercise 7, Part 2: Three.js and A-Frame Entities

In Part 2 of this chapter's exercise you will:

- Add Three.js code to an A-Frame application

- Create a Three.js TextureLoader to import an image asset

- Set the property values on a Three.js texture inside A-Frame

- Dynamically apply a Three.js texture and material to an A-Frame entity using JavaScript

- Access components of an A-Frame entity by using JavaScript and the DOM API to traverse an A-Frame's Object3D graph

Through the Window

By attaching the Three.js component to the window object, an object at the root of every Web page in a browser, A-Frame guarantees the Three.js library is always within reach. Beneath the frameworks and libraries we are still only working with JavaScript and the browser's built-in APIs. As a result, we may use the tools we've already sharpened throughout the exercises of this book to create a bit of custom functionality inside our A-Frame scene.

Three.js TextureLoader()

First, create an empty `<script>` tag between the closing `</body>` and `</html>` tags near the bottom of the index.htm document.

Then, create a Three.js `TextureLoader` object, load the brick texture from its folder, and store the value in a variable called texture.

```
<script type="text/javascript">
    const texture = new window.THREE.TextureLoader().load(
            'textures/brick_mat.jpg');
...
```

Though the use of the global "window" object is not required to access Three.js from an A-Frame project, I've used it in this step to illustrate how A-Frame maintains a connection with its source. Because the artifacting in our scene results from the compression and tiling of the brick texture, let's avail ourselves of Three.js' filtering tools to more efficiently render our data.

Three.js Properties in A-Frame

The filters we use to compress the texture applied to our cube's material are practically identical to those we used in exercise 4, part 3 in Chapter 5 about Three.js. They are available to us from within an A-Frame scene because of the global Three.js object, which we may access simply through the variable THREE, without the preceding call to the window object.

Texture Filters

Apply the desired filters to the texture stored in the variable.

```
texture.anisotropy = 16;
texture.minFilter = THREE.NearestFilter;
texture.maxFilter = THREE.NearestFilter
```

Because A-Frame retains access to the Three.js library through the window object, which is common to all Web pages, we may conclude that A-Frame also retains access to the browser window's APIs. One such API is the DOM API, which allows us to manipulate and reference elements in the structure of an HTML scene graph through attributes and classes.

Access the DOM API

Apply an ID attribute to the <a-box> primitive inside the scene and provide it with a unique value of your choice.

```
<a-box id="cubrick" position="0.3 1.5 -0.5" depth="0.5"
height="0.5" width="0.5"></a-box>
```

With our primitive A-Frame entity uniquely identified in the HTML scene graph, we can access it and its properties through familiar JS methods.

JavaScript Syntax in A-Frame

Create a new Three.js material and set as the value of its map property the brick texture we uploaded.

```
const material_tex = new THREE.MeshBasicMaterial({map: texture});
```

DOM Query

Query the DOM for the primitive we labeled and store its value in a new variable.

```
const box = document.querySelector('#cubrick');
```

With a reference to the A-Frame entity saved in a JS variable, we can access the underlying Three.js object through a method built into A-Frame entities.

Three.js Groups and getObject3D()

As we would like to set the material property of a Three.js mesh object, let's use the getObject3D() method built into A-Frame entities to access the underlying Three.js object by name.

```
const mesh = box.getObject3D('mesh');
```

A-Frame stores entities made-up of different Three.js objects in a Three.js data structure called a Group. By calling A-Frame's getObject3D('mesh') method on a variable that holds a Three.js Group, we are able to traverse the elements of the data structure to find the one matching the criteria of the string we passed as a parameter. Upon storing the <a-box> entity in a JS variable, we have effectively saved a reference to the Three.js Group that A-Frame wraps into its box entity.

Finally, with both the material and mesh stored in JS variables, we can complete the assignment of the brick texture to our cube.

```
mesh.material = material_tex;
```

As we are using a JS script to execute the import, filtering, and assignment of the material/texture to the <a-box>, we don't require any reference to it through A-Frame's HTML syntax.

Run the Scene

Before running the scene in the browser through your local development server, confirm that you have a) removed the Asset Management System entity from the top of the A-Frame scene, and b) removed the attributes on the <a-box> entity that refer to the brick texture.

Because A-Frame is a framework for Three.js, all the objects and behaviors in the Three.js library remain available to us within an A-Frame scene and project. Upon running the revamped A-Frame scene, you will see that the artifacting that had affected our cube's material texture has been corrected. Though A-Frame may not intrinsically offer built-in ways to amend the filters developers may like to apply to textures in their XR scenes, its consistent access to the global object THREE means the functionality of Three.js and all that it has to offer is no more than a keyword away.

Part 2 Recap

- Accessed the Three.js library through the global window object's property THREE

- Used traditional HTML attributes to define the ID for an entity in an A-Frame scene

- Used conventional JavaScript to access filter objects in Three.js

- Applied Three.js filters for mipmapping and anisotropy to an image texture

- Used the DOM API to reference an A-Frame entity as if it were a traditional HTML element

- Accessed the underlying Three.js objects of an A-Frame entity to dynamically set the texture property on an A-Frame entity's material component

Now that we've seen how A-Frame, as a framework for Three.js, retains accessibility to its underlying JavaScript source, we can move further ahead into the echelons of A-Frame's capabilities.

Custom Components in A-Frame

As an abstraction of JS syntax, A-Frame allows us to write pure JavaScript in its scenes. However, it also implements a feature of JavaScript that has become increasingly popular in the age of Web frameworks like React. As an ECS, A-Frame, under its hood, uses JavaScript components as the foundation of its system. Because components are universal to all applications written in JavaScript for the Web, not just those written with the A-Frame framework, XR developers can personalize A-Frame by creating A-Frame components of their own.

Exercise 7, Part 3: Build a Custom A-Frame Component

In Part 3 of this exercise you will:

- Create a custom component through the A-Frame registerComponent() function

- Learn how to store data in a custom component through a component's schema attribute

- Learn how to use life cycle hooks built into A-Frame components to schedule a component's behavior

- Use the 'this' keyword to access an entity's data from within an attached component

Setup

Let's begin Part 3 of this exercise by creating a new index.html page for our A-Frame project. Reset the starting code for the document by copying the following `<a-scene>` content and replacing the previous content.

```
<body>
    <a-scene>
        <a-plane id="ground" height="50" width="50"
         rotation="-90 0 0"></a-plane>
        <a-box position="0.3 1.5 -0.5" depth="0.5" height="0.5"
         width="0.5"></a-box>
        <a-sky color="#87CEEB"></a-sky>
    </a-scene>
</body>
```

registerComponent( )

To create a new, custom A-Frame component, we create a call to the `registerComponent()` method built into the A-Frame framework.

Within a new `<script></script>` tag in the `<head>` section of the HTML document, write the following stub:

```
    ...
    <script>
        AFRAME.registerComponent('texture-loader', {
            schema: {},
            init: function () {
                console.log('initialized');
            },
            update: function () {

            }
```

271

```
      });
   </script>
</head>
```

The first argument we pass into the registerComponent() method is the name we'd like to apply to our custom component. As we will reconfigure the JavaScript code we entered in Part 2 of this exercise, let's name our custom component 'texture-loader'.

schema

The structure of a custom A-Frame component follows a set of rules established by the framework. The schema keyword defines the attribute of the custom component which will hold as key/value pairs the data of the component. As we will soon see, the data of the component provides the information the component's functions will require to execute their duties.

init

The second attribute of the custom component is another built-in feature of A-Frame's registerComponent() function. The init attribute defines the behavior a component will perform upon its creation in an A-Frame scene. The value of the init attribute is a function, the body of which we will fill out with a simple console.log statement to notify us that the component has initialized.

update

The third attribute we've included in our custom component is another built-in attribute defined by the registerComponent() function. The update attribute defines the behavior the component will perform when any element of its schema undergoes a change. The update attribute also provides the convenient feature of executing the function to which it refers when our A-Frame scene instantiates the component. Therefore, any logic required by our component's initialization can live either inside the `init` or `update` attribute. Where we place the logic depends entirely on the aim of our component's purpose.

Custom Component Properties

Next, let's define the properties we'd like our texture-loader component to hold as data within its schema. Add the following properties as attributes within the schema's curly braces:

```
schema: {
    src: {},
    material_tex: {},
    mesh: {},
    texture: {}
},
```

While the values of the schema attributes are originally blank for our texture-loader component, their names will serve as targets to which we can dynamically set values in the bodies of A-Frame entities in our scene. However, before we define the values for the data in our component's schema, let's better understand how we plan to use the information we'd like our component to store.

Referencing Component Data From Inside the Component

JavaScript has a unique feature built into its language represented by the keyword `this`. Broadly, the `this` keyword in JavaScript refers to the object calling the method to which `this` is prepended or the object to whom the variable prepended by `this` belongs. For example, in our texture-loader component, we would like to store the texture created by a Three.js `TextureLoader` object in the attribute "`texture`" as defined in our component's schema.

'this'

In the update function of the `registerComponent()` function for our custom component, create a call to the Three.js `TextureLoader` constructor and save its output to the texture variable in the component's schema.

```
update: function () {
    this.data.texture = new THREE.TextureLoader().load(
        this.data.src
    );
}
```

The `this.data.texture` variable points to the texture attribute we defined in the schema for our custom texture-loader component. The "this" refers to the component itself, which we will attach to the `<a-box>` entity in our A-Frame scene.

Similarly, the `this.data.src` variable points to the `src` variable we defined at the top of our component's schema. Notice that we did not provide the variable `this.data.src` with a value, yet. The value for this variable will come from the entity to which we assign the custom component. To better understand this principle, let's add our custom component to an entity in our scene.

Add Custom Component to Entity

Add the name of our custom component, texture-loader, as a component to the `<a-box>` entity inside our `<a-scene>` tag.

```
<a-box texture-loader="src: textures/brick_mat.jpg"
       position="0.3 1.5 -0.5"
       depth="0.5" height="0.5" width="0.5"
></a-box>
```

Using the syntax of key/value pairs, we set the value of our component's src property as the relative file path of the image we'd like to import as its texture. Referring back to the first line of the texture-loader component's update function, we may see now that the value of the component's texture property will be the Three.js texture object created by loading the image at the file path stored within the src variable. Therefore, data passed into our custom-built texture-loader component through the properties defined in its schema object find their source in values we define within the A-Frame entity to which we attach our custom component.

With the value of the texture attribute set through the this.data. texture variable in our component's update function, we can access properties inherently provided by Three.js texture objects. As the value stored within the this.data.texture variable is the output of a Three.js TextureLoader, we know that the value is a Three.js texture object.

Three.js Properties Through Custom Components

Because the texture stored in this.data.texture is a Three.js texture object, we can access and define the properties inherent to Three.js textures, which we have already seen in this course's chapter on Three.js, Chapter 5.

Using JavaScript dot notation, access the anisotropy and mipmap properties on the texture value stored in the texture-loader's schema.

```
this.data.texture.anisotropy = 16;
this.data.texture.minFilter = THREE.NearestFilter;
this.data.texture.maxFilter = THREE.NearestFilter;
```

Here, we are only rewriting the code we wrote in the JavaScript <script> tags in the previous part of this exercise. As the purpose of creating a custom A-Frame component is to encapsulate the information required by a component, it should come as little surprise that we are relocating what was universally accessible in the previous part of this exercise into the confines of the texture-loader component.

Wrap It Up

Now that we have the source and properties of the texture object we'd like to wrap around our <a-box> element, we have only the remaining steps to execute: 1) apply the texture to a Three.js material; 2) acquire a reference to the Three.js mesh object wrapped by the A-Frame <a-box> primitive; and 3) apply the material and its texture to the <a-box> primitive.

Add Texture to Material

To apply the texture to a Three.js material, we place a call to a Three.js material constructor, set the component's src texture as the value to the material's "map" property, and store the material in the component's data.

```
this.data.material_tex = new THREE.MeshLambertMaterial( {map:
this.data.texture} );
```

Recall that the map property of a Three.js material is a built-in feature of the Three.js library. As a framework for Three.js, A-Frame easily allows us to create Three.js objects and store them in variables within A-Frame components' schema.

'this.el'

A-Frame provides a mechanism by which we can access any element or entity to which we add our custom component. By calling this.el and storing it in a variable within our component's update function, we provide our script the ability to manipulate the properties of the A-Frame element our component calls its parent.

Define a variable to hold the element to which we have applied our component.

```
const el = this.el;
```

The primitive <a-box> entity, like all entities in A-Frame, is a wrapper around a Three.js Group. A Three.js Group is like a scene graph or HTML syntax tree, a hierarchical collection of nodes that comprise a parent object. Through a call to the A-Frame method getObject3D(), we can access the individual Three.js objects that make up an A-Frame element.

Pass the Mesh

As most objects in Three.js have as their base class the Three.js Object3D class, we may use the getObject3D() method to access not only the underlying Three.js objects of an A-Frame element, but also the properties built into native Three.js objects.

Using JavaScript dot notation, access the Three.js mesh object on the <a-box> primitive and store it in a variable defined in our custom component's schema.

```
this.data.mesh = el.getObject3D('mesh');
```

With the <a-box> entity's mesh stored as a variable in our component schema, we can finally apply the brick material we loaded through the Three.js TextureLoader to the material property of the Three.js mesh of the A-Frame <a-box> entity.

```
this.data.mesh.material = this.data.material_tex;
```

With the texture and material finally applied to the <a-box> entity's Three.js mesh object, we can load the revamped HTML document in the browser through our local host development server.

Run the Scene

If all has gone according to plan, then you should see the same scene that loaded at the end of Part 2 of this exercise. The <a-box> entity in the A-Frame scene has been wrapped in a material the texture of which is the brick_mat.jpg file we loaded through our new, custom 'texture-loader' component. You can confirm that the component loaded the material and applied it to the entity by checking the browser's console for the "initialized" string we printed in the component's init function.

Part 3 Recap

- Created a custom A-Frame component using A-Frame's registerComponent() function

- Used a component's schema attribute to set the state of a component

- Used life cycle hooks built into A-Frame components to schedule behavior for the component's entity to perform

- Used the 'this' JavaScript keyword to get and set the data unique to an A-Frame entity's implementation of a custom component

Of course, loading the texture for a single entity in our A-Frame scene through a custom component doesn't make much sense, since the code we wrote in this part of the exercise was more complicated than the vanilla JavaScript we wrote in Part 2. However, the advantage of custom components, and components in general in A-Frame, becomes more apparent when we apply them to more than one entity at a time.

Two Birds, One Component

In Part 3 of this chapter's exercise, we created a custom component called "texture-loader" to both load and apply a texture to the material of an A-Frame <a-box> primitive. We replaced the generic A-Frame entity that held the geometry for a plane object with an A-Frame <a-plane> primitive.

```
<a-scene>
    <a-plane id="ground" height="50" width="50"
     rotation="-90 0 0"></a-plane>
 ...
```

In Part 4 of this exercise we will build out the functionality of the texture-loader to handle more than one case in our scene. Specifically, we will use the custom A-Frame component we created in Part 3 to load a grass texture and apply it to the plane that serves as the ground in our A-Frame scene.

Exercise 7, Part 4: Greener Pastures

In Part 4 of this exercise you will:

- Create a second instance of a custom component to attach to an A-Frame entity

- Expand the data stored by a custom component's schema to include new properties

- Apply both an image and normal map texture to an entity's material component

- Learn how to pass data into an instance of a custom component on an entity using A-Frame attributes

- Use conditional logic within a component's life cycle hooks to dynamically set the value of properties in its schema

- Add both a directional and ambient light source to an A-Frame scene

- Add fog to a scene as an A-Frame component

Add the Custom Component to a Plane Entity

Add the custom texture-loader component to the <a-plane> entity in our scene and set as its src the desired image from the project folder.

```
<a-plane id="ground"
         texture-loader="src: textures/grass.jpg"
         height="50" width="50"
         rotation="-90 0 0"
></a-plane>
```

Like the brick material we applied to the <a-box> entity, the grass.jpg image loads seamlessly into our A-Frame scene as a texture on the plane's Three.js material object. However, as the dimensions of our plane object are larger than our box entity, we have to apply certain Three.js texture filters to create a more balanced depiction of our scene. Let's begin by using the lessons we learned in exercise 4 from the course's chapter on Three.js, Chapter 5. As you may recall, developers may increase the believability of an XR scene by applying a normal map to an object's texture.

Add a Custom Component Attribute

To begin the process of adding a normal map to our plane's texture, let's define two new attributes within our custom component's schema.

```
schema: {
    src: {},
    material_tex: {},
    mesh: {},
    texture: {},
    normal: {type: "boolean"},
    normal_src: {}
},
```

Properties applied to the attributes of a custom component's schema in A-Frame provide developers with the option to define data types and default values for properties. To better understand why we'd use a "boolean" value to define the data type for an attribute that refers to a component's "normal map," let's return our attention to the logic of our component's update function.

Recall that one of the primary advantages of using a custom component in A-Frame instead of a traditional JS script is the reusability provided by components. By creating a single component with dedicated functionality, we can apply that component to more than one entity, thereby performing more work without rewriting any code. However, applying the same component to more than one entity in A-Frame should not limit developers from creating more robust behaviors for their components. One way we can diversify the performance of our custom component is through the introduction of conditional logic to its update function.

Component Diversity Through Logic

To the bottom of the code in the texture-loader custom component's update function, add the following if statement:

```
if (this.data.normal == true) {
    console.log('normal true');
    this.data.normal_map = new THREE.
    TextureLoader().load(
        this.data.normal_src
);
this.data.mesh.material.normalMap = this.
data.normal_map;
this.data.mesh.receiveShadow = true;
```

The logic that we've applied to the if statement in the texture-loader's update function is nearly identical in performance to the code we wrote in Part 3 of this exercise. The only difference in this code block is the conditional logic of the if statement. The schema attribute pointed at by the if statement is the boolean value we will pass through the component declaration in our scene's entity. If the value of the property is true, then the code in our update function will execute its body, which loads the image file we aim to use as our ground's normal map.

Passing Data as src

By defining the values for the schema attributes normal and normal_src in the body of the texture-loader component placed on the plane object in the scene, we are able to provide them as arguments to the component's update function.

Define the value of the normal and normal_map properties in the plane's texture-loader component.

```
texture-loader="src: textures/grass.jpg; normal: true; normal_
src: textures/grass-nm.jpg;"
```

Notice that we separate properties in the texture-loader component with semicolons, as we do with properties in CSS.

Of course, simply applying a normal map to the grass texture in our scene will not immediately transform the believability of the ground element. As we've already defined the anisotropy and mipmapping properties we'd like our texture-loader component to apply to whatever image it loads, we must write additional code to address the scale of the texture on the A-Frame plane.

Different Property Values from the Same Component

Again, we can apply the lessons we learned in this course's exercises with Three.js to edit the appearance of the texture on the plane object. Recall that the "wrap" and "repeat" properties are built into Three.js and are exposed on the Three.js texture object. Here, we set their values to the boolean value "true" in the texture-loader component on the plane object. As a result, they will become available as properties of the this.data object within the update function of our custom component's registerComponent() function.

Add two new attributes to the schema object in the registerComponent() function.

```
wrap: {type: "boolean", default: false},
repeat: {type: "boolean", default: false}
```

Since we've defined new attributes in our component's schema, let's set their values in the body of the texture-loader component we added to our plane object in the scene.

```
texture-loader="src: textures/grass.jpg; normal: true; normal_
src: textures/grass-nm.jpg; wrap: true; repeat: true"
```

At the bottom of the update function in the registerComponent() function, add the following conditional logic:

```
if (this.data.wrap === true && this.data.repeat === true) {
this.data.texture.wrapS = this.data.texture.wrapT = THREE.
RepeatWrapping;
this.data.texture.repeat.set(25, 25);
}
```

The logic of the if statement reads the values of the wrap and repeat properties we defined in the texture-loader component on our plane object. The body of the function sets the texture properties on the texture imported by the texture-loader, using properties inherent to Three.js. The value of the repeating property on the texture is not set in stone. You can change the value of the texture's repeating arguments to suit the style of your scene.

Saving and loading the scene in your browser will demonstrate the transformations executed by the custom texture-loader component on the default values of the imported image. One element you may not notice, however, is the role the plane's normal map texture plays in the scene. In fact, you won't notice it because it's not apparent.

The Lighting Model Persists

Because a texture's normal map responds to the lighting of a scene, we must provide the appropriate lighting objects to a scene to activate its normal maps.

To activate the normal map texture on the plane object in the A-Frame scene, add the following code to create both a directional light and ambient light to the scene:

```
<a-entity id="dir-light" light="type: directional;
color: #dfebff; intensity: 1" position="50 200 100">
</a-entity>
<a-entity light="type: ambient; color:
#666666"></a-entity>
```

Saving the HTML document and reloading the scene in the browser will hopefully demonstrate more realistic fidelity on the part of the grass texture's response to light. Adjusting the parameters of the light objects will better demonstrate the role played by the interaction between the object's normal map and the scene's lighting equation.

Fog as Component

Finally, we can add a last detail to our A-Frame scene by making use of an object familiar to use from Exercise 4, Part 3—fog. A-Frame provides convenient access to the Three.js fog object by exposing it as a component of its scene entity.

To add fog to our scene, we simply need to define the values for the fog component's properties built into the A-Frame scene element.

```
fog="type: exponential; density: 0.1; color: #cce0ff"
```

Saving the HTML document and reloading the scene in the browser will illustrate how easy it is to add fog to a scene through the A-Frame framework.

Part 4 Recap

- Created a second instance of a custom component and added it to an A-Frame entity

- Expanded the schema of a custom component to include properties for additional entities

- Added a normal map to an A-Frame material component as a Three.js texture

- Passed data into a component through an entity's attributes

- Used conditional logic within a component's life cycle functions to dynamically set the value of properties on an instance of the component

- Added a directional and ambient light source to an A-Frame scene

- Added fog to a scene as a component on an A-Frame scene entity

Summary

By now, you hopefully understand the tremendous support A-Frame provides developers for the creation of WebXR scenes. However, one feature of A-Frame we have not yet addressed is the manner through which it provides interaction between a user and an XR scene. In Chapter 9 we will avail ourselves of A-Frame's opportunities for customization as well as its built-in features, to implement a system that recreates real-world physics and create a component that interfaces with a user's XR controllers.

In this chapter you:

- Imported the A-Frame framework through an HTML script attribute

- Learned how an A-Frame scene entity handles and abstracts much of the logic required to launch both a Three.js scene and a WebXR session

- Created an A-Frame scene using primitive entities

- Used an example of an A-Frame system called the Asset Management System to preload an image asset required by a material component in a scene

- Wrote custom JavaScript to use the browser's DOM API to locate an A-Frame entity in an HTML scene graph

- Used JavaScript to dynamically load an image file as a Three.js texture and apply it to the material component of an A-Frame entity

- Used JavaScript to access the underlying Three.js objects on which A-Frame is built

- Dynamically set the values of Three.js texture properties to address artifacting and aliasing within a scene

- Created a custom component through A-Frame's `registerComponent()` function

- Set the state of a custom component through its schema

- Implemented logic and behavior within a custom component's life cycle hooks, such as `init` and `update`

- Dynamically applied both an image and a normal map to more than one instance of a custom component

- Learned the meaning of the `this` keyword when accessed within the functions of a custom component to get and set the state of a component's schema data

- Added a directional and ambient light to an A-Frame scene

- Added fog to an A-Frame scene as a component of the `<a-scene>` entity

CHAPTER 9

Physics and User Interaction in A-Frame

In our introduction to the A-Frame framework, we have focused on the entities and components that make up the heart of its Entity Component System (ECS). In A-Frame, entities wrap components to create complex objects in a 3D scene. While A-Frame provides developers with out-of-the-box entities called primitives (like a box, plane, cone, and sky), it also allows us to create entities of our own composed of custom components built through A-Frame. But the extensibility of A-Frame is not limited to entities and components. The virtues of A-Frame really take flight through the application of systems to its scenes.

In this chapter you will:

- Add a physics system to an A-Frame scene

- Use properties of an A-Frame physics system to apply real-world physics to entities in a scene

- Explore the A-Frame developer ecosystem for more custom-made systems and components to enrich our scenes

- Use the mixin feature of A-Frame to create a custom entity for VR controller interaction

- Use 3D models provided by A-Frame to create impressions of virtual controllers through which a user can interact with a scene

© Rakesh Baruah 2021
R. Baruah, *AR and VR Using the WebXR API*,
https://doi.org/10.1007/978-1-4842-6318-1_9

Where's the Game Engine?

Our journey through this course has been marked by an evolution of abstractions atop the WebGL API built into contemporary browsers. WebGL, we learned, is a graphics library for 3D objects on the Web; Three.js is a JavaScript library and API to facilitate with the rendering of WebGL scenes in the browser; and A-Frame is a framework built on top of Three.js. As we move up the ladder from primitive vertices compiled and rasterized through vertex and fragment shaders in WebGL, to entities and components in A-Frame, we see a workflow for creating WebXR that's increasingly simplified. One tool helpful for the creation of WebXR scenes and applications we have not addressed in this course is called a game engine.

There are entire books dedicated to learning the interfaces and workflows for game engines like Unreal, Unity, and Babylon.js, to name just a few. One feature these game engines uniquely provide that neither Three.js nor A-Frame inherently make available is a system of real-world physics. If you've ever designed an XR experience with a game engine like Unity, for example, you know that scenes almost immediately instantiate with the properties of gravity baked into the program. Gravity, of course, is an element of the physics of our everyday lives. The built-in availability of physics, like gravity, friction, and elasticity—collectively known as kinematics—is perhaps the main advantage of developing XR experiences with a game engine.

However, as we learned in the previous exercise, A-Frame is an extensible application; developers can create custom entities and components. Systems, too, are editable in A-Frame. Because systems that implement complex behavior like kinematics can be very difficult for an individual developer to concoct on their own, A-Frame is all the more helpful for providing us an ability to leverage systems created by other developers. All that we have to do is learn how to import them into our A-Frame scenes.

Exercise 8, Part 1: Importing a Ready-Made Physics System into A-Frame

In the previous exercise we learned how to create a custom component to add functionality to our A-Frame scene. In Part 1 of this exercise, we will make use of the A-Frame developer ecosystem to import a physics system already created, tested, and tuned by somebody else.

In this exercise you will:

- Learn about the scope of the A-Frame developer ecosystem

- Learn how to install an A-Frame package created by another developer into a scene you've created

- Access the properties of a third-party A-Frame package to create the illusion of real-world physics in an A-Frame scene

Install A-Frame and Systems

To begin this exercise, create a new HTML document with the A-Frame script import:

```
<script src="https://aframe.io/releases/1.0.4/aframe.min.js">
</script>
```

Then, visit the following link to find the A-Frame physics system add-on created by Don McCurdy:

`https://github.com/donmccurdy/aframe-physics-system`

Before you're alarmed at the prospect of importing a third-party script into your A-Frame project, it may help to speak a little about the A-Frame developer ecosystem.

A-Frame Developer Ecosystem

Created and maintained by Mozilla, A-Frame remains a free and open source framework for all who use it. Because A-Frame shares its source code with the internet, enthusiasts are able to create their own components and systems for the framework.

A-Frame Physics System

One of the most popular add-ons to the basic A-Frame starter project is the physics library created and maintained by one of A-Frame's cocreators, developer Don McCurdy.

1. Following the README.md documentation on McCurdy's GitHub page for his A-Frame physics system, we find the CDN through which to import the script into our project.

```
<script src="//cdn.rawgit.com/donmccurdy/aframe-
physics-system/v4.0.1/dist/aframe-physics-system.min.
js"></script>
```

The <head> section of your HTML document should now contain the following two scripts:

```
<script src="https://aframe.io/releases/1.0.4/aframe.min.js">
</script>
<script src="//cdn.rawgit.com/donmccurdy/aframe-physics-system/
v4.0.1/dist/aframe-physics-system.min.js"></script>
```

Load a System to a Scene Entity

Conventionally, to add a system to an A-Frame project, we provide the name of the system as an attribute on the A-Frame scene tag:

```
<a-scene physics="debug: false">
```

Turning the physics debug value to "true" wraps entities in the scene with wireframes that may help during development. The Readme.md file on the GitHub repository for the physics system has documentation for what other properties of the system you may access, such as the default gravity and friction for a scene. However, setting the value of the debug property to "false" and keeping the system's settings at their default values suits our needs during this exercise.

Add Physics Properties to Entities

To explore what an A-Frame scene with real-world physics applied can look like, let's add a camera, a plane, a sphere, and a box to our scene.

```
<a-camera position="0 0.3 0"></a-camera>
<a-plane material="color: gray" width="25" height="25"
rotation="-90 0 0" position="0 0.2 0" static-body></a-plane>
<a-sphere static-body position="-5 12 -6" material="color:
yellow" radius="2"></a-sphere>
<a-box dynamic-body grabbale position="0.5 50 -0.5"
material="color: blue" width="0.5" height="0.5" depth="0.5"></
a-box>
```

Most noteworthy in the code we added to our scene are the attributes called "static-body" and "dynamic-body." Coming from the physics systems we added to our <a-scene> entity, these attributes define the behavior of the objects in our scene. The "static-body" attribute in the physics system created by McCurdy defines an object that will not move. Conversely, an object identified as a "dynamic-body" will behave according to the physical laws defined in the scene, such as gravity and bounciness.

HTTP vs. HTTPS

Now, if you've tried to run the scene we've just built using the local development server that we have used throughout this course, then you may have run into an obstacle. As of this writing, no major Web browsers integrate with A-Frame to easily port a VR scene to a peripheral VR device through a computer. To test VR scenes created with A-Frame, one can use the Oculus Browser provided by the operating system of the Oculus Quest. If you are developing on a VR headset other than the Oculus Quest, refer to the documentation provided by your hardware's manufacturer to determine the best way to interact with an A-Frame application in a browser.

However, if you are developing an A-Frame scene through Oculus Browser with an Oculus Quest, like me, then there are two ways you can access your A-Frame content. As communication between a server and an Oculus Browser requires a secure, encrypted connection, we cannot directly access our development server through a Quest, even if ADB is running in our command prompt and a USB cable connects the device to our computer. To create an encrypted HTTPS connection on a local host server, you can either use GitHub pages or an application called Ngrok.

To create a personal page for your project on GitHub, visit the following link:

```
https://pages.github.com/
```

By registering for a free GitHub account, creating a personal repository, cloning the repository into your development folder, and adding the HTML document which contains your A-Frame scene, you can directly point your VR device's browser through GitHub Pages' HTTPS connection. We will walk through this process together in the next chapter.

If you aren't yet comfortable with the mechanics of GitHub, then, alternatively, you can download a package called Ngrok from NPM through the VS Code terminal.

```
https://ngrok.com/docs
```

As a free service, Ngrok provides a secure, encrypted HTTPS tunnel to the local host development server on your personal machine. Accessing an A-Frame scene through an Oculus Quest's Oculus Browser portal via the encrypted tunnel solves the security issues posed by a system's native HTTP connection. The major drawback to Ngrok as a free service, however, is that the encrypted URL pointing to your local development server will be randomly generated upon each startup. As the generated, encrypted link is difficult to memorize, it can be painful to type the address into a browser on a peripheral device. Paying a small subscription fee to Ngrok will allow you to create a personalized, encrypted URL that routinely points to your local host.

Once you've decided on an approach to encrypt the local host connection between your server and your VR headset, you are ready to launch the scene we created in Part 1 of this exercise.

Part 1 Recap

In Part 1 of this exercise you:

- Installed a physics system from the A-Frame developer ecosystem

- Attached a physics system to an A-Frame scene entity

- Attached properties of a physics system as attributes on A-Frame entities

- Used the "static-body" and "dynamic-body" attributes to mark entities as kinematic or not

Exercise 8, Part 2: Hands On

Of course real-world physics in a virtual scene doesn't mean too much if we or the users of our application can't experience the lifelike behavior for themselves. To really place us in the scene, to help us feel as if we are in another world, let's make use of both built-in A-Frame touch controller objects and another system available to us through the A-Frame developer ecosystem.

In Part 2 of this exercise you will:

- Import a system from the A-Frame developer ecosystem that specializes in touch interaction

- Connect both a third-party system and an A-Frame touch-controller component to create an XR touch-controller through the WebXR Gamepad API

- Learn to create A-Frame "mixins"

- Add interactive behaviors between touch-controllers and objects within an A-Frame scene through the application of collider objects, events, and filters

Super Hands

The Super Hands component is an A-Frame library created and maintained by Will Murphy. Murphy's Super Hands component conveniently packages the data, logic, and behavior required to apply touch-control interaction in an A-Frame scene.

Access Through GitHub

To import Murphy's Super Hands system, visit the GitHub repository:

```
https://github.com/wmurphyrd/aframe-super-hands-component
```

Import

Place the component's URL within a <script> tag in the <head> section of our HTML document.

```
<script src="https://unpkg.com/super-hands@3.0.0/dist/super-
hands.min.js"></script>
```

While Murphy's component adds interactivity between a user's controllers and objects in an A-Frame scene, it still requires the base behavior of A-Frame's built-in controller objects. A-Frame provides touch-controller entities for both Vive and Oculus touch controllers.

Touch-Controller Components

As I am developing with the Oculus Quest, I will add the Oculus-touch-controls component to a generic A-Frame entity.

```
<a-entity oculus-touch-controls="hand: left"></a-entity>
```

```
<a-entity oculus-touch-controls="hand: right"></a-entity>
```

Loading the scene in a VR browser like the Oculus Browser on the Oculus Quest, using an encrypted HTTPS link, will reveal models and textures with the appearance of Quest controllers tracking the real-time movements of your hands. Unfortunately, the touch-controller avatars cannot interact with the objects in our scene . . . yet.

Make it Interactive

To create the opportunity for interaction between the objects in our A-Frame scene and the touch controllers of our XR device, we must include one more component library developed by Super Hands creator Will Murphy.

```
<script src="https://unpkg.com/aframe-physics-extras@0.1.2/
dist/aframe-physics-extras.min.js"></script>
```

Building upon Don McCurdy's A-Frame physics system and his own Super Hands component, Murphy's A-Frame Physics Extras system acts as a bridge between our touch-controllers and the objects in an A-Frame scene.

A-Frame Physics Extra System

A review of the library's documentation on its GitHub repository shows that the Physics Extras system relies on the presence of a collider object on A-Frame's tracked controllers. To ensure that the controllers in our A-Frame scene contain all the attributes and components required by both Super Hands and Physics Extras, we can create an A-Frame object called a "mixin."

A-Frame Mixins

Immediately beneath the opening <a-scene> tag in the same HTML document from Part 1 of this exercise, create an opening and closing tag for A-Frame Asset Management System. Between the <a-asset> tags, create an A-Frame mixin entity with the following components and property values.

```
<a-scene physics="debug: false">
    <a-assets>
        <a-mixin id="controller"
            physics-collider
            static-body="shape: sphere; sphereRadius: 0.02"
            super-hands="colliderEvent: collisions;
                         colliderEventProperty: els;
                         colliderEndEvent: collisions;
                         colliderEndEventProperty: clearedEls"
            collision-filter = "group: hands;
                                collidesWith: blue;
                                collisionForces: false">
        </a-mixin>
```

The physics-collider and collision-filter components come courtesy of Murphy's Physics Extras library. The `static-body` component we import from McCurdy's A-Frame Physics library. The attributes for the Super Hands component come from Murphy's Super Hands script. You can learn the specifics of the Super Hands syntax and its built-in properties by reading the documentation on the component's GitHub repository.

Collider Events and Components

The collider, collider events, and collision filter components on the `mixin` encapsulate the functionality we'd like to add to our A-Frame touch controller entities.

We can add the mixin as a component to the controller entities inside our scene.

```
<a-entity oculus-touch-controls="hand: left"
model: true
mixin="controller">
</a-entity>

<a-entity oculus-touch-controls="hand: right"
model: true
mixin="controller">
</a-entity>
```

Of course, our controllers will do little to nothing without an object with which to interact in our scene.

Grabbable Attribute and Collision Filters

To create an interactable box object, let's add another mixin entity to the <a-assets> section of our scene. We can provide the objects in our scene with interactivity by adding the Physics Extra collision-filter component onto both the plane and the box object in our scene.

```
<a-mixin id="cube" dynamic-body grabbable
    geometry="primitive: box; width: 0.5; height:
    0.5; depth: 0.5">
</a-mixin>
```

We can then add the mixin to a new generic entity in our scene:

```
<a-entity mixin="cube" position="0 1 -1"
 material="color: blue" sleepy
    collision-filter="group: blue; collidesWith:
    default, hands">
</a-entity>
```

Finally, to make sure our new entity remains interactable with the ground in our scene, let's also add a collision-filter and physics-collider to the plane object.

```
<a-plane material="color: gray" width="25" height="25"
rotation="-90 0 0" position="0 0.2 0" static-body collision-
filter="collidesWith: blue" physics-collider></a-plane>
```

Saving the scene and loading it through your local host server via an encrypted tunnel will allow you to open it in the Oculus Browser inside the Oculus Quest.

Run the Scene

You should now be able to pick up the blue cube by gripping it with either one of your Quest controller avatars. To add additional grabbable objects to the scene, you can follow the steps taken in this part of the exercise, being sure to define the group and logic for the appropriate collision filters.

Part 2 Recap

- Added a touch-controller to a scene through the A-Frame touch-controller component

- Added functionality to the A-Frame touch-controller by importing and implementing the Super Hands component library

- Added interactivity between controllers and objects in an A-Frame scene by applying collider physics from A-Frame libraries accessible from within the developer ecosystem

- Used the underlying WebXR Gamepad API to interface between peripheral XR controllers and an A-Frame scene run in the browser

Summary

As you can hopefully tell by now, A-Frame is a unique application that helps Web developers create virtual reality scenes. Its HTML-inspired syntax and ECS sit atop tools with which we have become well familiar through this book. However, A-Frame's abstraction of the WebXR session request cycle, Three.js scene setup, and animation loop significantly reduce the amount of work and time a developer must dedicate to recreating boilerplate code. As a VR productivity tool, A-Frame has been hard to beat.

Despite its robustness out of the box, A-Frame does not offer all the conveniences an XR developer may expect from other productivity applications. Programs to make XR content like Unity, Unreal, and Babylon.js are souped-up Mustangs compared to A-Frame. As game engines, they contain nearly the entire pipeline of XR creation in convenient, contained environments. They also come complete with a physics system. Since most 3D games and XR experiences require kinematic properties like gravity, friction, and bounce, the physics systems built into game engines can be a real source of value for a developer. They can also create cost in the form of application size, complexity, and time for development. Because A-Frame is a framework for Three.js, not a game engine, it presupposes little but offers a lot.

Perhaps the greatest value provided by A-Frame is that it's open source. Not only is it free for us to use, but it also grows daily through its active, passionate developer ecosystem. Creating custom components and systems in A-Frame is straightforward—you've already done it—and anyone can share their work with others online. In this chapter alone, we recreated the physics of a game engine by simply importing a couple of scripts into an HTML document. If you've ever worked with the toolchain required by a game engine like Unity, then you probably already recognize the playful creativity A-Frame's simplicity can spark. As an open source project, A-Frame's purpose fits comfortably in the wider notions of the Web: creative, accessible communication for all. In the next and final chapter, we will stick with A-Frame, exploring what more it can offer when reality gets augmented with 3D models on our phones.

CHAPTER 10

Deploying 3D Animated Models in AR with A-Frame and GitHub Pages

Though we've nearly reached the end of our course on immersive AR and VR content using the WebXR API, we have only worked with primitive assets in XR scenes. Objects like cubes, planes, and spheres are helpful while we prototype experiences. However, creating an XR experience a user will enjoy requires a bit more imagination. One way we can increase the diversity of our XR applications is with 3D models.

While there are many different types of 3D models a developer can use in their XR scene, in this chapter we will focus exclusively on models encoded in the glTF format (GLTF). Like it does with OpenGL, the Kronos Group maintains the specification for the GLTF format. The purpose of the format is to conveniently standardize the use of 3D models in applications like those that implement the WebXR API.

In this chapter's exercise, the final in our series, we will build an augmented reality scene using A-Frame. The scene will include 3D models loaded according to the GLTF specification and animated with the help

© Rakesh Baruah 2021
R. Baruah, *AR and VR Using the WebXR API*,
https://doi.org/10.1007/978-1-4842-6318-1_10

of A-Frame's Animation-Mixer component. We will deploy the scene to a secure HTTPS site made available through a GitHub pages account. Upon completion you will have a mobile, augmented reality application you can open from anywhere through an AR-capable device.

In this chapter you will:

- Learn to create a secure, HTTPS development site using GitHub Pages

- Learn the fundamental commands to create, clone, and update a GitHub repository from VS Code

- Upload a GLTF asset through the A-Frame Asset Management System

- Access GLTF animation properties through A-Frame's Animation-Mixer component

- Place 3D models in an AR app that you can access from anywhere on a mobile device

HTTPS and XR Testing

As we've learned in previous chapters during this course, A-Frame is a framework that sits atop the JavaScript library Three.js. By encapsulating Three.js functionality into custom HTML entities, A-Frame simplifies the process of creating XR scenes through declarative HTML syntax. However, regardless of the conveniences provided through A-Frame abstractions, developing XR content from a local development server includes unique obstacles. One obstacle we've already encountered in exercise 8 is the challenge of creating a private, secure HTTPS connection on which we can test our XR applications.

GitHub

In exercise 8, I used the Ngrok application to create a secure HTTPS tunnel to my local host server. Perhaps you did the same. If you chose another route, however, it may have been through the version control application GitHub. Whether or not you are familiar with GitHub, together we will go through the steps of testing an XR application through an HTTPS connection provided by GitHub Pages.

Collaboration and Version Control

GitHub, itself, is a part of the Microsoft ecosystem. Yet, the service it offers is helpful regardless of operating system. At its core, GitHub is a version control software that facilitates collaboration on programming projects. While the scope of GitHub, as a whole, is too complicated to address fully in this short chapter, it does include basic features even novice developers can use. One of those features is the service it provides through GitHub Pages.

GitHub Pages

GitHub Pages, freely available with a GitHub account, allow developers to quickly create websites with a secure, encrypted HTTPS connection. Further, by connecting directly with a GitHub repository, GitHub Pages offer a development workflow free from third-party server applications. Anyone can access our GitHub Pages from the Web, if we choose to allow them to. A personal GitHub Page, in that sense, is more than just a local development server. But the quick, easy way it helps developers create HTTPS sites editable directly from an IDE like Visual Studio Code makes GitHub Pages an excellent resource for XR development and testing.

Exercise 9, Part 1: Upload a GLTF Model to A-Frame and Publish to GitHub Pages

In the exercise for this chapter we will set up a GitHub Page with a repository connected to our local development environment. Any changes we make in our HTML document, for example, will be accessible through HTTPS in the browser at our GitHub Page URL. We will, however, have to quickly review the few steps required by GitHub to create and maintain a repo. With our client-server connection set, we can proceed with creating an AR-enabled A-Frame scene that places a GLTF asset in our own environment. The source code and assets for this exercise are available on GitHub via the book's product page, located at `www.apress.com/9781484263174`.

In this exercise you will:

- Create a personalized GitHub homepage for HTTPS testing

- Clone a GitHub repository

- Load GLTF assets into an A-Frame project

- Place a GLTF model into a scene using an A-Frame component

- Use the transform components of an entity to manipulate a GLTF model in space

Set Up GitHub

To begin this exercise, we must first create a personal GitHub Page. The following instructions can be found on the official GitHub Pages documentation at `https://pages.github.com/`.

Create a repository

Head over to GitHub and create a new repository named **username.github.io**, where "username" is your username (or organization name) on GitHub.

- If the first part of the repository doesn't exactly match your username, it won't work, so make sure to get it right!

Clone the Repository

To clone a repository from GitHub to your local machine, you simply type the clone command into a terminal or command prompt. In a terminal or command prompt, navigate to the folder where you want to store your project, and clone the new repository:

```
~$ git clone https://github.com/username/username.github.io
```

Enter the project folder and add an index.html file:

```
~$ cd username.github.io
~$ echo "Hello World" > index.html
```

Push it

Add, commit, and push your changes:

```
~$ git add --all
~$ git commit -m "Initial commit"
~$ git push -u origin master
```

. . . and you're done! Fire up a browser and go to https://username.github.io.

GLTF Assets

Next, we will take steps toward adding a 3D asset to an A-Frame project.

Set Up Files

In the root file of your GitHub Pages folder in your IDE, create a new index.
html document and install the A-Frame library.

Add, Commit, and Push

To update the appearance of your GitHub homepage, you must first
add, commit, and push changes by repeating the steps described in the
previous section.

```
~$ git add --all
~$ git commit -m "[Your Message Here]"
~$ git push -u origin master
```

Download Course Assets

Download the 3D, animated GLTF models for this exercise from the course
files and save them in the root project folder of your IDE in a directory
named "assets."

Load GLTF Models

Using the A-Frame Asset Management System, load the GLTF models with
the <a-asset-item> A-Frame entity.

```
<a-scene>
  <!-- Asset Management System-->
  <a-assets>
    <a-asset-item id="dragon" src="./assets/dragon/scene.gltf">
    </a-asset-item>
```

```
    <a-asset-item id="city" src="./assets/city/scene.gltf">
    </a-asset-item>
  </a-assets>
  ...
```

GLTF-Model Entity Component

Create an empty <a-entity> tag in the A-Frame scene and apply the City model as the source for the entity's gltf-model component using the model's ID you assigned in the "GLTF Assets" section.

```
        <!--City GLTF model-->
        <a-entity gltf-model="#city"
        rotation="0 -90 0"
        scale
        position>
        </a-entity>
```

Model Transform Components

Set the values for the scale and position components.

```
        scale="0.0005 0.0005 0.0005"
         position="0 0 0">
```

Commit Changes

Commit the changes to GitHub with a comment. For example:

```
~$ git add --all
~$ git commit -m "Models added"
~$ git push -u origin master
```

Push and Publish

Push and publish the saved files to GitHub. Then, visit your GitHub homepage through your AR device's WebXR-capable browser, such as Google Chrome version 84.0.4.

Visit the URL

After saving the HTML file and pushing the stages to your GitHub repository, you will be able to navigate to the URL of your repo from a mobile device.

Access Permission

Select AR and provide the application permission to access the settings of your device. After saving the HTML file and pushing the stages to your GitHub repository, you will be able to navigate to the URL of your repo from a mobile device.

Run the Scene

The 3D model we added to the A-Frame scene should appear at the origin defined by your device. If your device is AR-enabled, then you may see an option at the corner of the screen to enter AR mode. Clicking on the button will activate the passthrough view of the device's camera and render the 3D model over the page. Scan your device around your environment until you locate the animated GLTF model.

And that's it!

Part 1 Recap

The GLTF format encodes and decodes the data comprising a 3D model through a syntax like JSON (JavaScript Object Notation). The key/value pairs in a model's `scene.gltf` file hold the same information we originally hand-coded into vertex and fragment shaders in exercises 1 and 2 of this book. By abstracting and automating the encoding of vertices into polygons and shapes, the GLTF specification helps developers create XR at scale. In Part 2 of the exercise we will add an animated GLTF model to our scene.

In Part 1 of this exercise you:

- Created a repository on GitHub Pages

- Cloned the repository to a local machine

- Initialized the repo with an index.html file

- Uploaded GLTF models using the A-Frame Asset Management System

- Placed a GLTF model in an A-Frame scene using the gltf-model component

- Set the transform values of a GLTF model through position and scale components on a generic entity

Exercise 9, Part 2: Animating GLTF Models in A-Frame

Artists may create 3D models in whatever program they prefer. Popular 3D modelling applications include Maya, Blender, and Zbrush, to name a few. Other programs exist too, which specialize in textures, materials, and animation rigging. Whatever platform a 3D artist uses to create their work, they can share it with the world through the GLTF transmission format.

In Part 1 of this exercise we imported a 3D GLTF model of a city. The model's `scene.gltf` file contained key/value pairs mapping the content, shape, size, and orientation of the model. But properties in a GLTF file do not exclusively refer to static elements of a model; the format also holds information describing the relationships between pieces of the model. Further, the GLTF format maintains spatially dependent data through transmission in a structure that remains quickly traversable by client-side algorithms. GLTF, therefore, is excellent for communicating animation to a scene.

In Part 2 of this exercise you will:

- Use the A-Frame Extras library to implement an animation-mixer component

- Loop through the animations baked into a GLTF asset using the animation-mixer component

- Define properties on relative transforms attached to unique models to create the illusion of an integrated scene

A-Frame Extras

Because a GLTF model we uploaded has animation data embedded into it, we can use a custom-made component called the A-Frame Animation-Mixer to animate the model in our scene. To access the component, we need only download the A-Frame Extras library created by A-Frame cocreator Don McCurdy.[1]

```
<script src="https://cdn.jsdelivr.net/gh/donmccurdy/aframe-
extras@v6.1.0/dist/aframe-extras.min.js"></script>
```

---

[1]Animation-Mixer component from A-Frame Extras library https://github.com/donmccurdy/aframe-extras/tree/master/src/loaders#animation

Animation-Mixer Component

Add the animated model to the scene and apply the animation-mixer component from the A-Frame Extras library to the entity.

```
<!--Dragon GLTF model-->
<a-entity gltf-model="#dragon"
scale="1 1 1"
animation-mixer
></a-entity>
```

Relative Transforms

Because we'd like the two models in our scene to coexist as if part of the same world, let's set the values of their respective transform components in reference to the same coordinate space. Set the value of the City model's position component to:

```
position=".07 1 -.5"
```

And the value of the Dragon model's position component to:

```
position="0.5 1.02 -0.7"
```

Like we did with the City model, we can also rotate the transform for the Dragon model.

```
rotation="0 270 0"
```

The value 270 in the rotation component for the Dragon model refers to a 270-degree rotation around the Y-axis, counterclockwise.

Commit

Commit the changes to GitHub with a comment.

Push and Publish

Push the saved files to GitHub and visit your GitHub homepage through your AR device's WebXR-capable browser.

Run the Scene

Select AR and provide the application permission to access the settings of your device. Scan your device around your environment until you locate the animated GLTF model. By moving your device around your environment, you will find the 3D model we uploaded to our scene animated in your space. As we've hosted the scene on GitHub Pages, you can access the scene remotely, too.

Part 2 Recap

Using 3D models in an XR scene is a sure-fire way to elevate the quality of immersive content. Because of the efficiency of the GLTF format, developers can import, upload, and send 3D models that boast fine detail as well as animation. By adding the A-Frame Extras library and employing its Animation-Mixer component into our scene, we quickly and conveniently created an animated scene. Further, we helped the scene seem whole by staging the models in reference to world coordinates. Deploying the scene to GitHub Pages through a repository cloned to our local machine, we even gave the scene life on the mobile Web.

In Part 2 of this exercise you:

- Uploaded a GLTF model with animations

- Imported the A-Frame Extras library

- Attached the A-Frame Extras Animation-Mixer Component to an entity with a `gltf-model` component

- Set the values of GLTF models' position, rotation, and scale components to create the illusion of a cohesive, animated scene in AR.

- Published the scene to GitHub Pages, accessible through the Web

Chapter Summary

A-Frame has shown itself to be a simple, powerful tool in the arsenal of the XR developer. Whether virtual or augmented reality, A-Frame provides the high-level convenience of creating XR scenes with both Three.js and the WebXR API. While some developers may prefer the freedom provided by vanilla JavaScript, others may enjoy the opinionated syntax A-Frame offers to rapidly create and iterate. Whichever camp you may fall into, outside of, or in between the complexity of encoding, transmitting, decoding, and presenting 3D content on mobile devices through the Web lends itself to the use of streamlined productivity applications like A-Frame. Of course, the Entity Component System or HTML-styled programming paradigm of A-Frame may not suit your preference. However, the framework's extensibility through customization and its easy access to the Three.js library on which it's built make A-Frame an evergreen option for novice and skilled developers alike.

In Chapters 8 and 9 we addressed A-Frame's capabilities as a framework for virtual reality. In this chapter we focused on the tools A-Frame offers for the creation of augmented reality applications. We also liberated our testing process by removing the USB tether between our devices and development machines. By hosting our application in a GitHub repository through GitHub Pages, we not only maintained a secure, encrypted HTTPS connection between client and host, we also allowed for the possibility of enjoying our AR experience remotely. Finally, we moved beyond primitive prototyping in our XR scenes and imported

3D models to provide detail and excitement. There is much left for you to explore about the GLTF format, 3D models, and animation in both AR and VR. Unfortunately, the landscape of XR is too broad and developing too quickly for this course to cover its breadth. It's my hope that upon completing this chapter and this course, you feel empowered, inspired, and enthused to continue learning and making XR for the Web.

In this chapter you:

- Created a personalized HTTPS connection through GitHub Pages

- Connected a local development environment to GitHub Pages through a GitHub repository

- Loaded a GLTF asset into an A-Frame scene using the A-Frame Asset Management System

- Used the add, commit, and push commands of GitHub to load an A-Frame scene to an HTTPS protected webpage

- Imported the A-Frame Extras library and used its Animation-Mixer component to loop through the animations baked into a GLTF model

- Manipulated the transform component properties of GLTF models to create an integrated scene

- Created a public webpage secured by HTTPS to test and share an AR experience created in A-Frame

Conclusion

We began this course with what may now, upon looking back, appear like a different time in a different world. From the practice of creating a basic 2D square in raw WebGL, we've arrived at a functioning augmented reality application. While on the journey together we also dove into Three.js and the different APIs leveraged by the WebXR API in the browser. These APIs included the WebXR AR module, the WebXR Hit Test module, the WebXR Spatial Tracking module, and the browser Gamepad API. In concert with more common, popular, but no less powerful APIs like the Document Object Model API and the Navigator API, we have been able to build XR experiences that range from the simple to the complex.

The aim of this book has been to not only introduce you to the creative tools exposed by the WebXR API but also provide you with a broad review of fundamental Web development practices. These practices include asynchronous programming, JavaScript modules, the Node Package Manager, closure, and scope, to name just a few. This book also led you on a tour of lower level technologies like GPU ALUs, WebGL, the HTML canvas compositor, and the OpenGL ES rendering pipeline. My hope has been to introduce 3D graphics programming to the Web developer, and Web development to the 3D graphics enthusiast. As the two fields continue to merge into the dynamic space of mixed reality development for the mobile Web, it is my sincere hope that you, upon completing the exercises in this book, feel empowered to leap into the bright, tumultuous, terrific future of immersive reality programming. After all, though the power to make new, alternative worlds lies within our grasp, we will never know another reality better than our own until people like you create it.

Index

S

T